John Bloomfield Jervis

The question of labour and capital

John Bloomfield Jervis

The question of labour and capital

ISBN/EAN: 9783337229528

Printed in Europe, USA, Canada, Australia, Japan

Cover: Foto ©Suzi / pixelio.de

More available books at **www.hansebooks.com**

THE QUESTION

OF

LABOUR AND CAPITAL

BY

JOHN B. JERVIS

(CIVIL ENGINEER)

AUTHOR OF "RAILWAY PROPERTY"

"The hand of the diligent maketh rich."

"He that gathereth by labour shall increase."

"Study a thrifty abstinence, and so aid in carrying forward a benign civilization."

NEW YORK

G. P. PUTNAM'S SONS

182 FIFTH AVENUE

1877

CONTENTS.

PREFACE.

THIS small book, which I now submit to the public, has been written with the view of showing that the young American working-man has the power of providing for his own well-being, and that there is no just ground of controversy between him and the capitalist. I have shown that under our civilization these parties must work together, and that this is for their mutual benefit. They are equally dependent on the market for the compensation they must receive for their respective wages and profits.

If the labourer refuses to work on this basis, he can have no wages; and if the capitalist refuses such profit for his instruments as the market will give, he will get nothing. The question is precisely the same as with a merchant who holds his goods above the market. Nor can there be any doubt in the case of services or goods, that the man who holds at a rate above the market, will not be able to exchange.

I have aimed to place the question in a practical light, with no partiality for either party, and earnestly commend my discussion to the study of all who may be interested in a question that is essentially involved in our civilization.

JOHN B. JERVIS.

ROME, N. Y., May, 1877.

INTRODUCTION.

THE question of labour and capital is a question of civilization. In the natural condition of men, —the untutored state,—the instruments of labour are hardly appreciable. They consist in such as are practicable, under their rude state, to facilitate the labour of hunting, fishing, and gathering of natural fruits. As man advances in intelligence, he by slow and gradual steps discovers new wants, and taxes his ingenuity to find the means of gratifying them. In regard to some certain thing that most presses his attention he contrives an improved method that facilitates his labour. One point gained, he finds the way opened for another. By continuing the process he steadily enlarges the scope of his instruments, until he reaches a demand that calls for the co-operation of several persons to provide the improved instruments he needs. This is a succinct statement of the progress of men from savage life to civilization. The history of mankind shows the process to have been a very slow one. As it has advanced, the necessity of law has been demonstrated. As property, or the instruments of labour were accumu-

9

lated, it became necessary to secure these as well as the rights of labour to the individuals who had acquired and who exercised these rights of property. It is only by this method that ingenuity, skill and labour can be protected, and every man secured in the results of his own labour, skill and prudence. It is manifest the inducement of endeavour is in securing to each man the possession and enjoyment of the product of his own labour and enterprise.

It can hardly be necessary to discuss the great superiority of civilization. A few remarks, however, may not be out of place, more especially relating to the benefits of civilization as connected with the instruments of labour. The first thing to consider is, the vast effectiveness of the instruments of civilization as compared with those of untutored men. This effectiveness of the former over the latter, it is not easy to estimate. I think it quite safe to put this estimate at fifty to one ; that is, the work of one man under civilization will produce what would require fifty untutored men to produce in the same time. But to avoid what to some may appear extravagant, put this ratio at ten to one, which is certainly very moderate. This shows that one man with the instruments of civilization will produce as much goods that are called for by the wants of men, as ten men in an untutored state. This result is reached by the skill and other instruments that have been provided by civilization.

If the higher classes of skill (not the highest) are equal to the labour, and all other instruments equal these, then we have the product of one skilled labourer as equal to that of ten untutored men. In many industries, and indeed in nearly all, the difference would be much greater; but we see in even this moderate estimate, how vast is the superiority of civilized over untutored labour in production. This is not a result for a few, but in all the arts that are engaged in fabricating goods that are wanted for the use of men. And not merely in the mechanic arts, but in those improvements that greatly increase the production of the soil. It is these circumstances in civilization that have raised the question of labour and capital. It brings into contest the labourer and the instruments of his labour. This contest cannot occur if the workman furnish his own instruments; but to a large extent the labourer depends on the capitalist to furnish the instruments, and here the contest enters. In the following pages I have aimed to show this must be adjusted in the same way as all commercial transactions are, namely, under the law of demand and supply.

The progress of civilization, or what is substantially the same thing, the useful arts, has advanced most rapidly in countries that were under free governments, or where civil liberty was enjoyed, and where freedom of industry has been alike secured to all, and no special favours by law or usage to any. It is the government most eminently beneficial to the working-man. It is in fact the only one under which he has a fair field to make the best of his industry; while at same time it holds him to his personal responsibility in providing for his own wants.

The object I have had in view in writing the following pages, has been to show that American working-men have a good field for their industry, and the power to provide for their own well-being. I should perhaps say young men, as no doubt many of the older members have passed the time and opportunity of their day. In regard to this position, it may be inquired—Have you fully considered the tendency of ignorance, prodigality and vice, that largely prevails among men, and the adverse influence these will exert to counteract your advice, and to break down the barriers you have raised? In reply, I am fully aware of the fact, that there are strong tendencies in the human mind to resist the best advice that can be given, and that these influences have so far prevailed as to give us a large class of dependent, and to no inconsiderable extent a degraded class of men.

On the other hand, it is beyond dispute that a large class of our American working-men, who had no other opportunities than those above mentioned, have reached conditions of comfortable independence and some of large wealth. Whatever may have been the circumstances that have given rise to the wide differences that have appeared, it cannot be claimed as arising from difference in corporeal power, or even in mental power. It has, beyond question, resulted from a difference in education and moral energy.

Looking back three centuries, at the condition of what was then regarded as the civilized world, what would have been said of a man who, at that day, should have predicted a state of society such as now exists in these American States ? Doubtless he would have been regarded by the ruling class of men as a fanatic—feeding on a wild imagination, and that the interests of society demanded the forcible suppression of his wild vagaries, as tending to disorder, anarchy and confusion. The progress from that day to this has certainly been slow ; the fanatics from time to time have been put down, but the truth that was involved, though covered by the dust that seemed to bury them and their principles, would take root and vegetate, spring up again and again ; men improving on each successive growth in their own knowledge of the great truths which at first they only saw dimly. At length the great truth, that man has "certain inalienable rights, of life, liberty and the pursuit of happiness," that no power of authority or usage has any right to meddle with or resist, came to be the great principle of Institutional law in these States of America. Thus the great principle gained a solid foothold. The prejudice of education and caste is not easily removed, and long-continued struggle was necessary to establish this great principle. It is, however, manifest beyond controversy, that progress has been made in the advance of truth, and we are encouraged, yea, warranted, to hope for its further advancement, in ways that will ameliorate the condition of men.

It is in this faith I have written this book, in the full conviction that the American young man, in either mental or manual labour, has the fairest field before him that has ever been enjoyed in any age or country, and that he is indebted for this to our civilization, whereby he is provided with the instrumentalities accumulated by the labour, skill and perseverance of his predecessors, making his labour vastly more productive for himself and also for society; all secured by the beneficent care and protection of our free government.

The great progress I have noted in ages that have passed, made against the general opinions of men, and under circumstances that gave no hope to any, except those regarded by common consent as dreaming and wild visionaries, affords good ground to hope for still greater progress, and for a large reduction of the ratio of the dependent class of men. At the same time I am well aware of the difficulties in the way of moral advancement, and do not expect very rapid improvement. But it is undeniable that, notwithstanding the impediments in the way, great and highly beneficial results have been attained, and we are therefore justified in the faith, that cultivation in morals and useful education, will carry us forward to a higher degree of civilization.

The great point is, to bring to the conviction of every young working-man the great truth, that he has the power to elevate himself and take his rank among independent men. To incite him to see, that what has been done by others he can do. It has been my effort to so discuss this subject that more or less of this class may see this, and so employ their powers as will not only improve their well-being in material means, but give them the character of upright citizens, fully able to maintain, improve and hand down to their posterity the great blessing of a high civilization. And

I hope in God my effort may be somewhat useful as encouraging young men to lay hold of the advantages that are before them, and by a manly energy secure their own well-being, and establish the character of upright and useful citizens. In this view I commend the following pages, and fully believe that many will consider my advice, and thereby realize my hope that my labour will not be in vain, and will tend to reduce the ratio of the dependent to the independent class of men. No doubt there are some who cannot be reached by any advice, and will still furnish material for, not only the dependent, but also for the degraded class.

Public and private interests are concerned in this question ; for whatever promotes the well-being of the individual, advances the public interest. In this view the public should provide for elementary education. Ignorance is the parent of indolence and waste, and these stimulate crime, and train up a class of men who are at war with society. The men who by diligent industry and prudence secure their own houses for residence and provide for the education and well-being of their children, are not found among those who congregate for schemes of dissipation, violence and plunder. Every one that can be added to the independent class, so far reduces the number of the dependent class, and thereby increases the safety, good order and prosperity of society.

The conclusions presented in the following pages have resulted from the experience and observations of a long life, in which I have had opportunity of extensive intercourse in the business walks of life, to notice the tendency of men in the conduct of their affairs. In this I have seen one man with no superiority of ability, rising to a condition of usefulness, independence and respectability, and another, with no lack of capability, except in the moral tone of his mind, failing to reach a respectable independence, and closing life in circumstances of want. The question is evidently a moral one, and though moral improvement is not readily made, it has been made—is practicable, and the only foundation for the happiness of men. I therefore earnestly commend this subject to the young working-men, as entirely within the reach of a manly enterprise and indispensable for their happiness. They have only to exercise the capability they possess, in a proper manner, in order to reach that degree of independence which gives character and personal dignity. If, on the other hand, they have not the moral nerve to improve their powers, they will inevitably, sooner or later, be compelled to take their place in the ranks of the dependent class. It is a question every young man must decide for himself, and if he choose the manly course, barring incidental circumstances that will sometimes be adverse to success, he will steadily rise to the condition of a useful and upright citizen, as all should do, in this free country, where every one has the full privilege to make the best of his situation.

The working-man has no just ground to be hostile to capital. He is aided in his work by the instruments provided by capital, as he will see by comparing the results of his labour with these in his hand, with what it would be, if no such instrument could be had. It will require but little reflection to see the truth of what the economist "About" says : "Capital is the instrument civilization has put in the hands of labour."

Capital is not an accident, nor in general the result of fortune. It is a thing acquired by what the "economists" call abstinence, that is, a man gathers by industry, and what he does not expend for any present use, he lays aside as an instrument for the future, regarding the present sacrifice as more than compensated by the beneficial use that will ultimately result from this abstinence. In this way he accumulates the instruments that facilitate or increase the productions of his labour. It may often be noticed as an observation of working-men, that the capitalists are fortunate men, and of those not capitalists, that they are unfortunate. No doubt there are circumstances that may and often do favour a man in the conduct of his labour. But in general these may be regarded as exceptional cases, when applied to large classes of men. In a country governed by Institutional law, or under civil liberty, where no class has, by law or usage, any privilege or right that is not equally enjoyed by all classes, there is no just ground of complaint on the part of any. All may succeed if they properly apply their powers. It is not fortune, but prudence and manly effort that makes the distinction.

As above noticed, it is very possible, and even probable, that one man may enjoy in some way superior facilities that may favour the productions of his labour. But this only accounts for a difference in degree of success. It is still true as a general proposition, that the capitalist reaches his position by the diligent, prudent and economical conduct of his affairs. He sets out with a purpose to improve his well-being, and, with patient perseverance in his mind and labours, in due time reaches the result he had purposed. This course, under free government, is equally open to all men. If this is correct, why then do so large a proportion fail to improve it? If one class of men reach so desirable a condition of independence, why not all?

That some do not reach this condition, arises from the fact they are not willing to practice the industry and abstinence necessary to secure the benefits of their own well-being. It is not always the case, that the latter class are indolent or incompetent. They have industry and capacity for business, but they are in too great haste for results—have not the patient perseverance that can wait and restrain their desires. The slow and steady gains of well-directed industry and frugal habits, do not satisfy their ambition. The process appears too slow, and with a view to hasten to their goal, they engage in speculative operations, and not uncommonly outside of their regular calling, entering a field they have not properly surveyed, and of course very likely to lose what they may have gained. If one unsuccessful attempt would cure them, and bring their minds to return to and diligently pursue their regular calling, it might be expected they would profit by the development of their errors. But this rarely happens, and the resistless appetite for rapid gains tends to throw into the shade, if it does not destroy, the hopes of regular industry ; and so they go from one failure to another, until all relish is lost for the steady gains of industry, and their lives end in failure. It often happens this class are intelligent men, able to discuss affairs so well that their friends wonder why

it is they do not succeed ; — that so much ability
should fail, and want instead of prosperity should be
the result. The cardinal difficulty in their case is,
they eschew the methods that experience has marked
out, and hasten by an untried process to reach results
that can only be obtained by systematic and patient
perseverance.

In this land of Institutional law, capitalists are the
men who have accumulated by saving. It is in this
way they have provided the instruments of labour for
their own use, and for the class who have not practiced
the necessary abstinence. These instruments are
only accumulated under Institutional law, where every
man is protected in the enjoyment of his own labour
and enterprise. Without such protection there can
be no adequate security, for no man accumulates if
he is in danger of spoliation ; consequently under the
apprehension of being deprived of their enjoyment,
no such instruments can be had, and men must be
content to do the best they may without them. There
is no escape from this.

What the working-man, as he enters on his career
of industry should regard, is the fact, that these instruments of civilization are a great benefit to him. He
finds them at his hand ready for use, and it is his interest to make the best use of them he may be able.

It will be in his power to accumulate these instruments to a certain extent as his own, and this by the same means the capitalist accumulates them before him. So far as he does this he will enjoy the profits of his instruments in addition to the wages of his labour. If the instruments are too expensive for the means of the workman, he must depend on some capitalist who has provided them. In the latter case the workman must pay the capitalist in the form of interest or profit for their use. This is simply justice, and precisely what the workman will expect from his junior workmen, when he himself has become the capitalist.

On the other hand, let the working-man consider wnat would be the situation if no such instruments had been provided. He must go back to the uncivilized condition of society, where no such instruments were known. How shall he appreciate or comprehend such an alternative as this? It is hardly possible to impress the force of this contrast on the mind of any man, surrounded by civilization, when no such alternative is seen. The idea of making goods by a process that would require a hundred men to do the work of one, cannot be realized under our existing civilization. If, then, the instruments are so important, it is certainly reasonable and just they should receive a profit commensurate with the value of the abstinence that was necessary to provide them. This is precisely what the working-man will expect, after he has accumulated the instruments by his own abstinence or saving.

If there could be any possible ground to doubt the utility of the instruments, it should be carefully examined and exposed. The fact that all prudent men make the exertion of abstinence, in order to procure them, is ample evidence of their usefulness. It is simply because they are an aid to industry, that they are provided or used at all. No workman is compelled to use them, nor does he use them, except so far as he regards them a benefit in the productiveness of his labour, that inures to his own advantage. Why then does the workman complain of an instrument that increases the benefits of his own labour by amplifying his product? He does not complain of the instrument in itself—but claims, that he should have some portion of the profits of the instrument, in addition to the wages of his labour Here is the manifest injustice of the claim, and it is at the basis of the conflict between labour and capital. The instruments and the labour are equally in the open market. The workman can command the instruments he needs, at the market rate, in the same way he commands the market rate for his labour. In the

one case tne labour is sold, and in the other the instrument is sold, and both are exchanged on the basis
of the law of demand and supply. Neither party is
compelled to contract, and only enter on engagement in view of what they regard as a measure that
will promote their respective interests.

The instrument is a necessity, for the reason
that it is a means of production, without which the
labourer would be unable to accomplish his work
except at a greatly increased amount of labour, and
this would be manifestly adverse not only to his own
interest, but also to that of the public. It cannot be
a question as to whether the instrument shall or shall
not be used ; its importance in production is too
manifest for this to be entertained, and the only
question that has been involved in this conflict is, the
relative wages and profits, as between the workman
and the capitalist. These parties come together to
negotiate terms for their respective services, and
stand on the same footing as any parties engaged in
buying and selling commodities in all commercial
exchanges. In the following discussion I have aimed
to show that this transaction between labour and
capital is precisely the same as that between any
buyer and seller, and has no claim to be regarded in
any special sense as a conflict, or more strictly a con-

test. It may be said in general of all commercial negotiations, there is often more or less of contest, and that between labour and capital is neither an exception nor a peculiarity. They are all governed by the one law of demand and supply.

LABOUR AND CAPITAL.

THE question of labour and capital, or their relation to each other, has of late been very much discussed on the platform, in the public press, and by formal treatises. The idea very generally entertained has been, that there is something wrong in this relation, which needs in some way to be adjusted.

In the existing organization in civilized communities, labour and capital are united in the various works of production. In so far as the workmen and capitalist are the same persons—furnishing their own capital and doing their own work, there can be no controversy: wages and profits go to the same parties. The main question in this discussion is with labour and capital as two parties in production. The one receiving compensation in the form of wages, and the other in profits or interest on the capital. The point at issue is,—that the labourer does not receive his proper share in the fruits of production.

It is important to have terms well understood. Writers on industrial economy have very generally, I

27

believe, treated the term "labour and capital" as the
proper designation of the relation in which the employer stands to the employed.   In his " Treatise on
Wages," Professor F. A. Walker does not assent to
this term.   On page 289 he says: " The true wages
question is the question of employment.   Hence the
popular phrase, ' the contest of labour and capital,' becomes at once revealed as a misnomer.   The true
controversy is not between the labourer and the capitalist, but between the labourer and his employer, to
whom labourer and capitalist are compelled to resort for the opportunity to produce wealth and derive
income." . . . . " The employer, the *entrepeneur*, stands
between the capitalist and the labourer, makes his
terms with each, and directs the courses and methods
of industry with almost unquestioned authority.   To
labourer and to capitalist alike he guarantees a reward
at fixed rates, taking for himself whatever his skill,
enterprise and good fortune shall secure."   As this
proposition of Professor Walker upsets a long-estab-
lished term as a " misnomer," it may be well to
examine it.   The argument goes to establish the
employer as a common contracting party between
labourer and capitalist.   It is obvious that in some
way the employer must make terms with the capitalist
for his funds.   The supposition is, the employer has

no capital of his own ; if it were otherwise, he would
be the capitalist. How then is he to contract with
the capitalist ? Certainly he must have security to
offer for the funds he requires to carry on his work of
production. It cannot be supposed the capitalist will
contract his funds without security. If the employer
gives security, it must be because he has the property
necessary for such security, or he must have a character so high the capitalist will furnish the funds on
the character of the employer. In the first case, it is
evident the employer is the capitalist ; in the second,
the capitalist takes the risk of the enterprise on the personal character of the employer, and a failure of profits
will fall on the capitalist who furnished the funds.

The idea of Professor Walker is, I think, that
capitalists do not go into production on the basis of
profits, but on the basis of loan to producers. Now it
is obvious there must be a party that can furnish
funds for the business of production ; and these funds
can only come from capitalists. If the capitalist furnish funds, direct, for any work of production, depending on the profits that may arise from such use of
his capital, then there can be no question he is one
party in the work of production. If the employer has
the funds, or the ability to furnish them on his own
security, then he is clearly the capitalist, and the

only party interested in the profits. In the latter
case the capitalist who may furnish funds or loans
looks to his securities for interest and the re-payment
of his funds, and has not necessarily any interest in
the profits of the enterprise.

In any light in which this question can be viewed,
I see no escape from the conclusion, that in some way
there must be capital furnished on the basis of remuneration from the profits of the enterprise. If I
am right, then capital must be strictly one party in
production ; and I see no more appropriate term for
this discussion, than " labour and capital," as the two
parties involved in this question. If, as in some cases
claimed, the labourer waits for his pay until his
product is marketed, then the labourer, so far as his
wages is concerned, is the capitalist, and sustains
himself on his own means for the time being.

The employer, in the sense presented by Professor
Walker, must not be confounded with the person of
superintendent. The latter is employed by the capitalist not for his capital, but for his skill as an expert in
conducting the kind of production they engage in. In
this capacity he employs labour, and conducts the
affairs of the enterprise under the general advice and
instructions of his principals. In this sense he
may be regarded as an employer of labour.

WAGES FUND.

Economists have taken the ground there was a "wages fund" from which wages were paid. In their discussions, they assume no wages can be paid beyond the resources of this fund. That if one class receive a greater proportion than their share, others will receive less. In the discussion of this subject in his treatise on "Political Economy," page 159, Professor Cairnes says: "As I understand this passage (quoting from Mr. Mill), it embraces the following statements: 1st, Wages is a general term, used in the absence of any other more familiar, to express the aggregate of all wages at any given time in possession of the labouring population; 2d, On the proportion of this fund to the number of the labouring population depends at any given time the average rate of wages; 3d, The amount of the fund is determined by the amount of general wealth which is applied to the direct purchase of labour, whether with a view to productive or unproductive employment." On page 160, he further states: "Our analysis thus leads us to the result, that the passage quoted from Mr. Mill cannot be taken to contain controversial matter. The statements are such as may not be disputed, once their meaning is clearly understood. At the same time it must be frecly confessed that it contains no solution of the wages problem : it is not a solution, but a statement of that problem—a statement, as it seems to me, at once clear, comprehensive, and succinct, presenting in clear light the two factors which constitute the phenomenon—the wages fund resulting from the direct demand for labour, and the labouring population forming the supply. The solution will consist in connecting these factors with those principles of human nature and facts of the external world which form the premises of economic science."

I do not see any objection to the statement of Professor Cairnes in the three propositions above stated, nor in the paragraph at the close of the second of the above quotations. But if, as he states, "it is not a solution but a statement of the problem," I can hardly appreciate its practical value. There appears a difficulty in ascertaining the value of the factors, without which no definite solution could be reached. No doubt the funds for wages must be obtained from capital, and that an increase of capital tends to increase the funds applicable to wages, and this may or may not affect the rate of wages, that depending on the supply of labour at the time.

For a doctrine that has been so largely accepted, and discussed with much ability, it is certainly singular that it has not taken a shape to admit of distinct solution. What can be the value of the theory of the " wages fund," if we cannot ascertain what the amount of the fund is ? How can we make available, or reach a dividend when the value of the factors is not known ? I am not aware that any one has attempted to establish any rule or process by which it could be determined for any country, among the numerous complications of its industries, what amount had been set aside or estimated for wages. The wages that had been paid in any country, may be ascertained for some previous year, though in the vast complications of numerous industries, this would be attended with great difficulty. So far as ascertained they would be a guide as to what the " wages fund " may be for the next year. At best, that I can see, this would be only an approximation ; and considering the changes that frequently occur, by which one industry would be increased and another diminished, could hardly afford a basis of definite determination for any particular industry for the ensuing year, what the rate of wages should be ; which is the solution sought.

Professor F. A. Walker (" wages question ") has discussed the " wages fund," and regards it as no solution of the wages question. He is the only author I have met who takes exception to the doctrine of a " wages fund." For the following reasons I consider

Professor Walker correct in the conclusions he has drawn. First, I see no practicable method of ascertaining what amount of capital may at any time be set aside as a fund for the payment of wages. Second, if the aggregate fund could be ascertained, I see no way that a disposition of the fund could be so apportioned to each of the numerous industries as would determine the rate of wages in each. The circumstances that affect the market for products, must influence the rate of wages, rising at one time with one branch of production, and falling with another. If this is correct, it leaves the "wages fund" as no solution, or of no practical value in determining the rate of wages at any particular time for any special industry.

So far as I can see, the doctrine of a "wages fund" has no further value than that an increase of capital may be regarded as tending to increase the ratio of its appropriation to objects of production. In this, capital will seek those industries that promise the best profit.

Wages Paid out of Capital.

In his discussion of this question, Professor Walker takes the ground that wages are paid out of production, and not out of capital, and therefore there can be no

" wages fund." No doubt the production is relied on as the ultimate resource for the payment of wages ; but I think it a very general practice to pay wages before the product is available, and certainly the avails of production in such case must be anticipated by the appropriation of capital. If a labourer can support himself until his product is marketed, he then furnishes the capital necessary for his support, while he labours for his wages. So far the labourer becomes the capitalist. This is the case with all labourers who furnish their own capital. Farmers, especially in the employment of single or unmarried men, by the season, often pay at the end of the season, the farmer furnishing the board or living of the labourer. If the labourer has a family to support, the farmer will generally be re- quired to advance on his wages, if he does not pay monthly.

In manufacturing industry it is the general practice, so far as I have known, to pay labour semi-monthly, or monthly ; and as the goods made cannot be marketed so as to realize the proceeds until some months after the labour is performed, capital must come in for the payment of wages. No doubt there are manufac- turers who do not pay in this prompt manner, and sometimes resort to the method of truck or store pay, a method not to be commended, and always indicating a dependent condition of the labourer. But as before stated, when wages is deferred, the labourer so far becomes the capitalist, supporting himself until the product is marketed.

I concede the proposition, that production must pay both wages and profits, though capital is necessary to anticipate wages until production can reach a market. This is true, whether the labourer furnish it himself, or it be furnished to him by his employer.

COMPETITION AND MARKET.

In the transactions of men for the sale and purchase of goods, competition and the market will rule their trade. To illustrate: let A desire to make purchase for a certain class of property that is held by D, and if E and F hold on sale the same class of property, A will avail of the competition that may be offered by D, E and F to obtain a favourable rate. This is obviously favourable to A ; but if A, B and C desire to purchase, and there is only D that has that class of property on the market, then the competition will be in favor of D, and he will obtain the highest price that either A, B or C may be willing to pay. In either case, the rate will be settled by the supply and demand for that particular class of property or goods on the market. However far apart the parties may com-

mence negotiation, they will come at what they understand to be the market rate, before they close the
transaction. It is immaterial whether the negotiation
is on a cash or credit basis. Parties in such negotiations
are very likely to look each to his own view of the
market, and thereby produce much contest, in supporting their respective views. But however they
contest that the seller cannot afford the goods at so
low a rate, or the buyer that he cannot afford to pay
so high, if they consummate the transaction, it will
be on the market value, whether under competition or
not. Here we see the general method of business,
though in many cases there is so little disparity
of opinion as to the market value, that little or no contest is experienced. Men of business will not waste
time in contest over what they know to be the market
value ; so well is it understood as the basis of all regular business transactions.

In the above remarks, it is understood, the parties
stand on an even basis, and no peculiar advantage held
by either. Notwithstanding it is a contest or conflict
more or less severe, according to the position of the
respective parties and their appreciation of the condition of the market, it rests on the law of supply
and demand, and though one or the other may complain, it is submitted to as inevitable when the transac-

tion is closed.   No one complains of this, and in fact no other rule could be substituted.

Is there then any reason why the negotiations between labour and capital should not be adjusted on the same principle as in the case above stated between buyer and seller ?   The capitalist desires to purchase labour on the best terms the market will allow, and the labourer sells his labour for the best wages he can command.   If there is more work to be done than labour to perform it, the competition will be in favor of the workman, and the market in his favour ; on the other hand, if there are more workmen than work, capital will have the advantage.   The case is clearly parallel to that of buyer and seller—resting on the same basis of competition and the market value of the commodity in question.

To this it is replied, the parties in the case of labour and capital do not stand on an even footing—that labour is dependent on wages for the means of subsistence, and thereby compelled to accept what capital may offer.   No doubt there are numerous cases in all departments of business where the parties to an exchange do not stand on an equal basis of independence. One of the parties may be under pressing need, that brings his negotiations under restraint, and compels him to yield to terms that under freedom he would not consent to; but notwithstanding such cases, no one thinks of changing the basis of exchange, leaving every one to reap the benefit of the favourable circumstances that he may find in his negotiations. The rule is one of general acceptance, that a man is justified in concluding the best bargain the condition of the parties and the market will permit. It is impossible to establish any other rule—it is founded on the principle that man is a free agent endowed with power and ability with the duty of taking care of himself. Under this rule an article is worth what it will command on the market. This is precisely correct, though the article in trade may have cost more. This certainly offers no excuse for any deception that may be attempted. But it is charged that the capitalist takes advantage of the labourers' necessities, and this gives all the force there is to this controversy on the question of wages, as in conflict with capital

In his elements of "Political Economy," sixth edition, Professor Perry on page 136 says: "Capital does not like to lose its profit any more than the labourer likes to lose his bread. In a true and general view, the one is under just as much pressure to employ labourers, as the other to get employment. They come together of necessity into a relation of mutual dependence, which God has ordained, and which, though man may temporarily disturb it, he can never overthrow." It will be noticed, this view of Professor Perry places the parties on the basis of equality in their negotiations. But while this is true, Professor Perry seems to admit the existence of circumstances that give capital an advantage, though he places the blame on the labourer, as at page 140, he remarks— " It is not denied that capital takes advantage of the ignorance and immobility of labourers, and sometimes secures their services at a less rate than the just relations of capital and labour then and there would indicate ; but the remedy for this is not in arbitrary interference of government in the bargain, but in the intelligence and self-respect of the labourers which shall fit them to insist on a just bargain. In this whole sphere of exchange, the just and comprehensive rule always will be, that when men exchange services with each other each party is bound to look out for his own interest, to know the market value of his own service, and to obtain the best terms for himself which he can make. Capital does this for itself, and labourers ought to do this for themselves, and if they are persistently cheated in the exchange, they have nobody to blame but themselves. Government should give them all facilities for intelligence : they should give themselves a character, and cherish a hearty self-respect, which there is nothing in their position to diminish ; towards such labourers, capital occupies no vantage ground in an exchange of mutual services."

The substance of the above quotation is, that the laws of trade must govern in the exchanges of labour and capital, same as in other exchanges, and that the labourer must depend on himself to obtain a standing of equality with capital. Tacitly, it is an admission the present condition of labourers does not in general maintain this equality.

Professor F. A. Walker, in his "wages question," page 291, remarks : " Since, then, the employer gets his profits only as the labourer gets his wages, and because the labourer gets his wages it is difficult to see that the employer is any more necessary to the labourer than the labourer is to the employer, or that either has any *natural* advantage over the other." Again, at page 295, Mr. Walker says : "We do not, then, find any ground for attributing to either employer or labourer a natural advantage over the other." Notwithstanding these positions, in alluding to the poverty of labourers, which he says is not universal but very general, on page 297, makes the following remark : " They are, therefore, unable to stand out against their employers and make terms for their services, or to seek a better market for their labour in

another town or city, but must accept the first offer
for employment, however meagre the compensation."
. . . " They lack the primary physical means of sustaining that contest."   At the same time Professor Walker
sets forth reasons to show that capital has a strong
interest to yield to the workmen in the contest.   He
discusses with much fulness and fairness the circumstances of the two parties.

In regard to the labourer, Professor Walker sets
forth the difficulties in regard to mobility, as a reason
the labourer is not able to avail of the competition for
labour in other towns than the one of his residence.
Though the expense of mobility is greatly less in
regard to time and money than it was half a century
ago, it is no doubt serious to most labourers, and as
Mr. Walker discusses it, a great impediment to securing the benefit on the part of the labourer of general
competition.

This subject is discussed under a somewhat different aspect from either Professors Perry or Walker,
by Professor Cairnes in his " Political Economy."
Professor Cairnes at page 233, says : " I hold that, at
least in countries in which the industrial and commercial spirit is strong, the power of capitalists by
combination to depress wages or to keep them down
is not a whit more real than that of workmen by

similar means to force them up. Either may, no
doubt, effect their object for a time; but neither, as I
believe, can be permanently successful." In his
further discussion he points out the difficulties under
which labour is placed, and makes the remark page
285—"I am, therefore, on this point at one with the
socialists; but while I agree with them so far, I am
wholly unable to accept the means which socialism
proposes for effecting the required elevation. The
leading idea in most schemes of socialistic reform is
the notion of raising labourers from dependence on the
labour market by throwing on society, in the person
of the State, the duty of providing them with capital.
Now by whatever means it is sought to give effect to
this idea—whether through the mechanism of a State
Bank," "or by loans without security," "one and
all are open to the objection of doing violence to
the principle of property, the weight and scope of
which objection I have already sufficiently insisted
on." On page 287 Professor Cairnes says : " Keeping
this object in view, I think it should at the outset be
clearly laid down that there is no royal road to the
possession of capital. Capital can only be created by
saving, and, where people have not saved themselves,
can only be honestly obtained by offering to those
who have saved, an adequate inducement in the form

of security and interest to prevail on them to part
with it.   If, then, the labourer is to emerge from his
present position and become a sharer in the gains of
capital, he must in the first instance learn to save."
This advice of Mr. Cairnes is excellent, and should
be fully considered by every labouring man, and especially the young.

After pointing out the means the labourer has for
effecting savings, Professor Cairnes, at page 289, says :
" To say this, however, is by no means to say that
the labouring classes, as a whole, are now prepared to
enter on this path, or that any very great change in
our modes of carrying on industry can soon or easily
be effected.   I am   far   indeed from thinking so.
But here again I desire to point out that the obstacles
in the way are not physical, are not even economic,
but moral or intellectual ; or if economic, only in so
far as economic results depend on intellectual and
moral conditions."   From the above it will be seen
Mr. Cairnes' hopes are not very strong for improving
the condition of the labourer.

Mr. Washington Gladden, in his book on " Working
Men and their Employers," has discussed the question
of labour and capital in a very practical manner.   Mr.
Gladden frankly examines both sides of the question,
and finds merit and fault with each party.   It is, how-

ever, obvious that he is under the impression there is
some hardship towards the labourer that ought to be
ameliorated; but he places his hopes of this on the
basis of moral and intellectual culture. Mr. Gladden
has large hopes from co-operation, and none at all
from communism. His book may be read with profit
by both working-men and capitalists; and I hope it
may have a large circulation. His discussion of the
influence of intoxicating drinks is very sensible, and
should not fail to exert a highly favourable influence.

In the recent work of Mr. J. N. Larned, "Talks
about Labour," I find some curious propositions, making the labourer a very impotent member of society.
Mr. Larned says, page 23: "Here, then, entangled
helplessly in the meshes of the vast net-work of this
modern organization of labour and exchange, stands
the man who has hands and brain, intelligence, strength,
and will to work, according to the demand of nature,
for what he needs, but who stands empty-handed
— with no accumulation of things hitherto produced—no capital. What can he do? There are no
wild creatures any more within his reach that he can
hunt for food, or whose skins he can appropriate for
clothing. There is not an animal that he can kill
which is not the property of somebody—stamped with
the right of possession by acquirement or accumula-

tion." This is certainly singular language in a country in which labour is free, and the rights of property secured to all who are willing to practice the industry and frugality by which all property is accumulated. It is evident Mr. Larned is at war with the existing system of labour, regarding the labourer as suffering from the oppression of capital, or from the accumulation of others. But he has not left the subject quite so bald as this,—not quite so ready as it would seem, to abandon civilization and take to hunting for animals that belong only to those who can take them.

At page 44, Mr. Larned says: "First of all, there is the capital that has been accumulated in the hands that hold it by industry and economy; by hard work, producing as much as possible, and by saving or unwasteful habits, consuming as little as may be." This is sound economy. Mr. Larned goes on to discuss other methods of acquisition, which he approves in part, and condemns in part; it is not necessary to follow these, as we are discussing the relations of labour and capital, and the admission above quoted shows Mr. Larned to believe that accumulation may be by labour and saving.

Mr. Larned says, page 75 : "A man cannot be a good artisan or mechanic in any kind of hand-labour which makes the least demand upon intelligent faculties, without concentrating so much of all his powers upon the immediate object of his labour, that he is compelled to trust its ultimate results, so far as his own benefit is concerned, to other agencies." This is certainly taking from the labourer all hope of improvement by cultivating his intellect, except so far as this may be brought to bear on the article he manipulates. Still, Mr. Larned is evidently engaged in an effort to promote the elevation of the labourer ; though it is difficult to see how this can be done by any other means than by the elevation of the labourer in mental and moral culture.

Again, on page 78, Mr. Larned says : " I am convinced that the desertion and deterioration of mechanical industries will continue to be an increasing evil until we have begun in some way to cut down the excessive premiums which our present adjustment of the relationships between capital and labour puts upon those faculties and energies that enter into what we distinguish from other labour by calling it business." The idea of Mr. Larned appears to be, that labour does not get its due share in production. The remedy called for by him is a union in some way between labour and capital, by which the labour will participate in the profits of capital. If I understand him, the plan of organization for production is to be such that the labourer will have some portion of the profits of capital in addition to his wages. It is obvious this claims for labour something beyond the market value of wages out of the profits due to capital ; in other words, the labourer is to have some portion of the profits due to the instruments, though he has not accumulated any portion. It must be remembered that under our organization of labour, wages is paid before anything goes to profits of capital, and if the production is unprofitable, capital must first lose. The labourer does not lose unless the capitalist fails, and consequently loses all profits. This feature in our organization of labour should not be lost sight of. It is clearly in this feature the labourer has the advantage over the capitalist.

In any production that may admit of being worked on shares, by which a certain part is to go to the labourer, and a certain part to the capitalist, there can be no objection to the method of providing specifically what portion each shall have. In such case the risk of loss would fall equally on both. In the work of farm production, this share plan is often adopted, as when a capitalist furnishes a farm and contracts with a tenant to receive in lieu of rent, a certain share of the product. This is often done in agricultural affairs, but in that case the tenant supports himself and provides the labour and materials necessary to cultivate the farm. In fact the tenant must have some capital, and of consequence a portion of the instruments of his labour.

At page 80 Mr. Larned says : " One becomes naturally the employer, and one the employed, instead of each being the employer of the capabilities of the other on fairly adjusted terms. One receives his daily rate of wages, fixed for the most part by the average state of need in his class ; the other makes what he can out of the bargain, and drives it hard to make the utmost. It is very plain to me that no equity in the partitioning of the products of human industry can be had under the wages system that we now maintain."

It will be noticed that Mr. Larned rests his plan for the improvement of the labourer on some method of contract with the capitalist, though I do not see that he specifies the method to be adopted, as to how these parties are to form this co-partnership or contract for production. From his discussion of the proposition it is evident he does not consider the world has yet reached that point of civilization necessary to carry out his idea. Speaking of the time it will require to educate men up to his system, or ideal system, he says, page 96 : " I do not expect it very soon. I am not sure we are within ten centuries of it yet." This is certainly " hope deferred." It may be that some men

4

may work under the impulse of such a hope, but it seems important to examine the matter very carefully and see if it be not possible to find a more speedy solution.

It will be noticed, the authors I have quoted mainly direct their attention to discover some benefit to the labourer which they suppose he does not now enjoy. I shall have occasion to make further reference to them in the following pages. In the mean time I earnestly recommend to all who desire to follow this subject, a careful attention to their discussions. Though I do not assent to all the positions taken in those treatises, they will be found of great interest and value on the important subject of industrial economy.

From the authors quoted I make the following

DEDUCTIONS.

First.—That under our present civilization, the productions required to supply the wants of men must be obtained by the united application of labour and capital.

Second.—That the union of capital and labour involves a competition between these parties, as to the wages and profit to each, in the same way that pertains to all transactions in exchange.

Third.—That owing to his condition of dependence, the labourer does not stand in this competition on an even basis with the capitalist.

Fourth.—That the capitalists (with many exceptions) are disposed to avail of their advantage, and drive the closest bargain with the labourer that circumstances may permit.

Fifth.—That the hope of the labourer rests mainly on the culture of his moral and intellectual faculties.

Sixth.—That under our present civilization the relations of labour and capital must be determined by the laws of trade, or supply and demand.

Seventh.—That hope is entertained, though for the most part faintly, of benefit to the labourer from co-operation ; depending on his improvement in intelligence and self-control.

Eighth.—That no benefit can result from any government interference or control, other than in maintaining justice ; that the organization and prosecution of industrial enterprise is most effective under the scrutiny and supervision of individual control.

On these several deductions I remark, First deduction—" That under our present civilization, the productions required to supply the wants of men must be obtained by the united application of labour and capital."

This implies the co-operation of two parties in

production, who come together to arrange the amount that shall be paid to the labourer as wages, for his part in the production contemplated. In any discussion of this relation it is necessary to understand the characteristics of the respective parties; for though they are in union in respect to production, they evidently have interests in conflict, however these interests may be harmonized to mutual satisfaction. The simple fact is, one party furnishes the skill and labour of manipulation, and the other the instruments of labor.

It must be kept in mind, that in the process of civilization it has been discovered there are certain instruments that greatly increase the efficiency of labour. These instruments are produced from the accumulations of previous labour, gathered from the savings of industry and frugality. The motive for collecting these instruments is, that they are productive of profit or income to the owner. They consist in land, buildings, machinery, tools, power to operate the mill, raw stock and the wages of labour that must be provided before the avails of the product can be realized. The capitalist relies on his net product to compensate him for the use of his capital and his personal supervision of the business. It is clear he will not engage in industrial enterprise unless he believes there is fair prospect of his receiving profits that will be considerably more than his funds would command on loan at interest.

I will endeavour to state the relation of the parties. This will involve the " Second deduction."

In going into an industrial enterprise, the capitalist incurs risk. First, the elements may injure or destroy his works ; or injury and loss may occur to other parties so as to effect his interest indirectly. Secondly, various circumstances may affect his production, making it more expensive than he had anticipated. Third, the state of the market may change, so that when his product is offered for sale, its value may be less than he had anticipated, and instead of showing profits, may show a loss. All business men know these contingencies enter into all sound calculations in starting an industrial enterprise, especially those of the larger class, of which I am here considering, and in which the question of labour and capital is particularly involved. The capitalist will naturally look for at least the prospect of profits that will indemnify him against the hazard he must take. Some industrial enterprises have resulted in large profits to the capital ; but it is well known that many prove very unfavorable ; so much so that capitalists are cautious in committing their funds to this kind of investment, and especially the class of large capitalists, who generally prefer to loan on interest, even at a much less rate than would be regarded reasonable in industrial enterprises. However strong the confidence of the capitalist in the profits he anticipates, he must take the risk involved in such enterprises.

In the progress of constructing the works, the capitalist has employed much labour ; but now they are completed and ready for operation, and he will require labour of more or less varied character, to conduct his production. This labour he must have, or his mill will be unproductive. He knew this before he began his enterprise, and based his estimates on what at the time was regarded the rate of wages for the work he needed. For the further illustration I proceed to consider the

SECOND DEDUCTION—namely, " That the union of capital and labour involves a competition between the parties, as to the wages and profits for each in the same way that pertains to any other transaction in exchange."

Now, the works having been erected, the parties enter on the negotiation for labour. The capitalist cannot command the labour without the consent of the labourer, and the labourer will insist on the market value of his labour. The capitalist has no alternative ; the labour he must have or his enterprise must be abandoned as a failure. If he will not pay the market price for labour, he has no power to command it. The idea involved in this is the dependence of the capitalist on the labourers required to operate his production. Only under a system of slavery could this be otherwise, and such a system does not exist under this government. We could not always say this—but thanks be to God! we are now free from legal slavery, that is, personal slavery; and every man has the right to dictate his own terms for his services. I am aware of the objection that will be urged against this position; that there are circumstances which give one man so much power over another, as to compel submission of the weaker party. This point I propose to consider in the course of my discussions.

As previously stated, the capitalist has completed his works, and is ready to go into operation for the contemplated production. The parties that must co-operate in the enterprise, having entered into negotiation for the wages the labourer must have for his part in production, they do not discuss the profits that shall accrue to the instruments, but the value of the labour as established at the time in the labour market. It follows, of course, that if the number of labourers that seek employment in this particular branch of work are numerous, the rate of wages will be low ; if, on the contrary, they be comparatively few, the wages will be high.   This is the inevitable condition of these parties, and their negotiations will be adjusted or settled on this principle.   It is the business aspect as resting on the laws of trade, that pertains in this, as in all business exchange.   The charitable view that is sometimes urged, I propose to examine hereafter.

The rate of wages will be affected by the skill required, the severity of the work, its hazards to injuries, and its general influence on health.   It is not necessary to discuss these at this time, as they are all subject to the general law of supply and demand, according to their respective influence on the rate of wages.

It is natural and legitimate for each party to conduct this class of negotiation on the same basis of interest that controls in all contracts for services. Each is his own guardian, naturally and properly, and will be prompted to secure the most favourable result for himself.   If the laws of trade are cheerfully accepted, the parties will proceed in harmonious cooperation, and the best practicable result in the wages and profits will be realized.   The only objection that I have noticed to this basis of action is, that the workman is less independent, and less intelligent than the capitalist.   Certainly the capitalist cannot be censured for this, and it is not to the credit of the workman that it should be so. If the labourer looks fairly at this case, he will see that it would be impossible for him to perform the kind of work contemplated without the instruments the capitalist has provided. If the labourer looks at the subject with intelligence, he will see the capitalist of this generation was the labourer in the past generation; and if he exercises the same diligence, prudence and frugality, he may expect to be the capitalist of the next genertion, or at least to such an extent as will place him in competent independence. I speak particularly of this country, where no right or power of entail secures family possessions; where every one is at liberty to pursue the branch of labour he prefers, and is secured in the full enjoyment of his own earnings.

It is strictly true that the capitalist has come to his position by saving from his earnings. Some have reasoned against this, and contended that capital has mainly been accumulated by speculation, by inheritance, or by unjust and fraudulent means. No doubt capitalists have been made by speculative operations, and not always just—that fortunes have been obtained from inheritance, and that fraud has been an instrument of accumulation. What the relative proportion in amount of these may be to the total of capital, I have no means of determining, and can only estimate them from observation. That from inheritance arises mostly from the savings of parents or other friends, from their industry. It is no doubt true that unscrupulous men do sometimes become large capitalists; but my observation convinces me, and I think it will appear so to those who explore society, namely, that by far the largest number of our capitalists, as well as those who obtain a competent independence, commenced their business life with little or no means but their industry, intelligence, and prudence to depend on. This should be, and will be, an encouragement to every industrious, prudent and enterprising man. I know from experience what it is to be a labouring man, and I most unhesitatingly say to every working-man, take the best offer the market will give you, and go to work with confidence in your ability to reach the success of the capitalists that have gone before you, and with manly effort overcome and not succumb to the difficulties that only demand a reasonable energy to clear your path; giving no heed to the platform and other literature that sets forth your condition as one of impotence and hopelessness, calling for some amelioration that is not consistent with your manhood.

I have been thus particular to show that there is **no**

natural advantage of one over the other, in the negotiations between the capitalist and the intelligent and (as he should be) independent labourer.

REMARKS ON MY THIRD DEDUCTION.

Namely—" That owing to his condition of dependence, the labourer does not stand in this competition on an even basis with the capitalist."

In the preceding remarks, it will be noticed that some reference is had to this point. It may be generally regarded as practically the condition of the working people in the class more especially employed in the larger establishments of production. So far as this is true, it no doubt arises from a necessity of obtaining prompt exchange for labour, and the want of intelligence and mobility or the part of the labourer. The argument in this case is, that the labourer is in need for his current subsistence, and therefore compelled to take what the capitalist may offer. That the labourer cannot delay his negotiation to a more favourable state of the market, for the reason he has starvation before him. While the capitalist, it is presumed, can wait for such change in the market as will best promote his interest. Now as these parties must come together, and as both have interests to serve, they cannot long delay on the question of wages unless the enterprise be abandoned. Neither desire this, and they will eventually agree on the basis of the actual market, if they agree at all. Naturally they are on even terms ; at the same time, I think it often happens that the capitalist, from his resources in means and intelligence, has an advantage in this species of exchange. So far as this may be an evil, it calls loudly on the labourer to so cultivate his means and his intelligence, as to qualify him to maintain his independence, and secure by manly energy the full market value of his services. The labourer is one party in the negotiation, and if he fail to secure success, it is for him to see the cause of failure to fully obtain the value of his services. The market value is all he can obtain, and it is for the interest of the workman to make the best of this.

Remarks on my Fourth Deduction.

Namely—" That the capitalists (with many exceptions) are disposed to avail of their advantage, and drive the closest bargain with the labourer that circumstances may permit."

In this respect it cannot be doubted there are two classes of capitalists. The *First class* are those who conduct themselves towards their working people in a spirit of uprightness. They wisely and kindly con-

sider their situation, and fully meet all their engagements with them. They cannot eschew the fundamental principles of business, but will kindly consider any
untoward condition of their working people, and extend such relief and sympathy as they may be able.
In their intercourse, they will treat their work people
with a courteous deportment, not failing any occasion
to say a kind word to encourage and cheer them in
their work, losing no opportunity to give them good
advice in relation to their personal affairs. In this the
capitalists have not only the pleasure arising from such
course of conduct, but the satisfaction of commanding
the best class of working people the market may
afford ; and they may expect the least waste in tools
and material, and, consequently, the most efficient
workmanship. In regard to the market value of
wages, they will look upon the subject with a just
regard to the interest of the labourers, while they
exercise a discreet regard to the business aspect of their
production. They know they cannot neglect the latter
without ruin to their enterprise.

The Second Class of Capitalists are those who have
very little sympathy for their working people. They
hold themselves aloof from the labourer, and if they
perchance extend any civility, it will be with an air of
condescension not pleasant to an American workman.

Their demeanor will usually indicate a standing quite too far above the labourer to admit his self-respect, and at times they treat him with a severity not at all necessary for any business object. This class regard it necessary to be severe, and hold a dignified eminence among their work people, as a party dependent on the patronage of the capitalist, in obtaining their bread. They enter into no sympathy for the consideration of those circumstances of hardship that naturally call for the aid of kindness. In regard to wages, this class hold rigidly to what they regard the business aspect of the question, and when there is a plethora in the labour market, they are able to command terms that are strictly severe on the labourer. It does not require argument to show that this class of capitalists will not generally obtain the best class of working people. They depend on the vigilance of supervision, and not so much on the character of the workman, to secure favourable results. They generally pay with promptness (though sometimes on the truck method); for the wages is the only motive of the labourer. The latter has no inducement as to the fellowship of his relations. The administration of this class may be strictly just, but certainly will not attach their work people, so as to produce any special regard for their interest. The labourers will have no particular regard for the success of the enterprise, except so far as it promotes their own interest.

The "*first class*" of capitalists will appreciate the good opinion of the public, as the same will arise from their just estimate of uprightness, and their cordial fellowship in sympathy for the just and proper rights of men. This will naturally draw to them the best class of work people. The "*second class*" of capitalists will not much heed public opinion, though they cannot wholly disregard it. They will be compelled to accept such workmen as cannot find employment with the first class. In any event they will only obtain such workmen as, from whatever circumstance, are willing to accept conditions of more or less severity, and will be constantly exposed to lose the best workmen, as they find opportunity for employment on more satisfactory terms.

It is not to be understood the "first class" of capitalists will not govern their affairs mainly with reference to the business object of their enterprise. They will not lose sight of this, nor is it to the interest of the workmen that they should. They know it is indispensable the business be conducted so as to provide both wages and profits, or it will of necessity be abandoned. All intelligent workmen know this, as well as the capitalist.

The question in regard to the power of the capitalist is not confined to the negotiations between him and the labourer, but is equally operative in all his transactions in exchange. If he drive a sharp contract with the labourer, he will be equally sharp in contracting for materials or the sale of his goods, as he may have occasion in the course of general business. There is, therefore, no propriety in making this a specific question as between labour and capital. Whatever there is in this question, is a demonstration of the power of capital to secure the most favourable exchange the state of the market will allow. No man should complain of this, but rather regard it a stimulus to pursue those means of intelligent industry and prudent management of his affairs which will secure it. It must be kept constantly in mind that it has been by these means the capitalist has secured the advantage of his position ; and what has been done by one may be done by others, having the same energy and self-control.

Remarks on my Fifth Deduction.

Namely—"That the hope of the labourer rests mainly on the culture of his moral and intellectual faculties."

There can be no dispute of this. The race of men are so constituted, that improvement in any respect must result from personal or individual effort. There is no other path than this. The institutions that give free action to the individual, and maintain the just rights of all, offer the best basis for the well-being of every one. Under our free government, the field is open, and the means adequate, for the improvement of those powers God has given us, to provide for all our wants ; and those who improve these powers will secure the blessing, and those who do not, have no right to complain of those that do. The labourer will profit by exercising self-control, and without this, there is no hope of rescuing him from a state of dependence.

Remarks on my Sixth Deduction.

Namely—" That under our present civilization, the relations of the labourer and the capitalist must be determined by the laws of trade, or supply and demand."

Whatever sentimentalists may urge, there is no escape from this position. It is a natural law, and will not yield to any pleading. The seller may contend he cannot afford to sell at less rate, and the buyer that he cannot afford to pay the rate demanded. It is obvious that numerous circumstances might be offered in this debate, of which the respective parties may have known very little ; yet they will, notwithstanding, refer to and be controlled by the value of the commodity in the market. This justifies no deception, and there may not have been any in the negotiation. The simple fact in the case under consideration is, labour is a commodity the labourer desires to sell, and must be governed by the same law that pertains to other property offered for exchange. Its worth is precisely what the market will command. It is simply for the labourer to decide whether it be for his interest to accept the offer that he may have, or look elsewhere for a market. On any business basis it is impossible to conduct industrial enterprise on any other principle.

Remarks on my Seventh Deduction.

Namely—"That hope is entertained, though for the most part faintly, of benefit to the labourer from co-operation ; depending on his improvement in intelligence and self-control."

I say "faintly," for the authors I have quoted, while they seem to regard co-operation as opening the best prospect to the working class, do not disguise their opinion that in the present condition of our civilization, the labourers in general

have not the moral and intellectual quality necessary for the successful management of industrial
enterprise on anything like a large scale, without the
experience of capitalists for executive, or purely business affairs. In this I think they are substantially
correct, but not fully so. I have confidence that the
labourers will rise, to a large extent, to such improvement of their powers as will give them the full
benefit of their labour, whether it be by co-operation
or otherwise. This question will be discussed more
fully under the consideration of methods and facilities for the improvement of labourers.

Remarks on my Eighth Deduction.

Namely—" That no benefit can result from any
government interference or control; that the organization and prosecution of industrial enterprise,
is most effective under the scrutiny of individual
control."

There can be no doubt of the soundness of the
above. It is no part of the function of government
to meddle with the affairs of individuals, except to
secure the administration of justice. It is the duty
of government to protect every man in the rights of
labour and enterprise, and take care that no wrong
that may be attempted, shall fail of adjudication on the

basis of justice, and that no one shall hold a privilege not secured to all. When governments attempt to interfere in the affairs of individuals, and dictate as to their rights of labour and exchange, they transcend their functions, and injure all labour and enterprise, and, in fact, vitiate the legitimate duties they were established to promote.

The latter clause in the eighth deduction, namely, " That the organization and prosecution of industrial enterprise is most effective under the scrutiny of individual control," is equally manifest. There can be no doubt the organization of labour and the administration of the operations of production is best done by an individual who has an experimental or expert knowledge of the processes of his work, and has, or is able to command, the capital required. The next best, or second in order of efficiency is, for two or three such persons to unite in a co-partnership, and by their united capital, industry and skill, conduct the process of production. The third in order is the incorporation of so considerable a number of members as to require a board of managers to conduct their affairs. In the last there is danger of inefficiency, and of side issues that are adverse to the joint interests, and which are often prosecuted under pretense of serving the general good of the company.

The difficulty in such cases is, the proprietors are not in a situation to understand well the methods by which their own affairs are conducted, and will mainly depend for success on the wisdom they exercise in selecting their agents.

If we leave the department of productive enterprise, and look into affairs necessarily committed to government, and trace along up from municipal to State and Federal administration, we shall have abundent evidence, as we ascend from the least to the greatest, of a regular advance in improvidence, waste and peculation. The great difficulty in government operations is that they are mostly out of the observation of those who by taxes pay the expense; and cunning men make their living by watching their opportunity to prey on the public, through managing rings and other processes. But in government affairs we have no alternative—we must commit the work to be done to representatives, and in their intelligence and honesty we must confide. In this we are sometimes successful and obtain faithful servants; but it is certain we often fail. We have no such necessity in the business of production.

In view of the fact that the great majority of mankind must obtain their subsistence from the wages of labour, it is of great importance to investigate the plans or methods that have been proposed or may be proposed to ameliorate the circumstances and as far as possible remove the obstacles to their happiness.

In any view of the labour question, we must not lose sight of the fact that there is a large amount of the productions of exchangeable commodities that do not require more capital for their favourable production than may be commanded by a single workman, or the combination of two or three in working partnership. So far as this extends, there is no contest between labour and capital. Enterprises formed is this way, with small comparative beginnings, frequently grow from the industry and prudence of the men, and so by degrees enlarging the scale of production from their savings, to ultimately reach large dimensions, employing labour as in all large industries. Such move out of the class we are particularly considering. This discussion having special reference to that class of working people who have little or no instrumentalities to aid their labour, and must depend for these on the capitalist, I now proceed to consider the methods that are looked to for their benefit. I commence this by some general remarks, with a view to show the condition of the respective parties, after which I propose to take a view of such measures as have been proposed to improve the condition of working people.

REMARKS ON THE GENERAL CONDITION OF THE PARTIES.

In all the affairs of business there is more or less of competition, especially with those of the same class. Every producer aims to secure a profitable market for his product. This is a wholesome struggle, bringing out the best results—tending greatly to the public good, in supplying the market with the best and cheapest articles required for consumption. This competition calls out and puts in operation the best method of production. It is the same in the labour as in the completed product. It embraces not only production, but transport, exchange, and professional service. In all these, labour, skill and capital are combined, and the best result is obtained when these are conducted in harmony, and are most eminent in degree. All exercise their powers and facilities in view of the law of supply and demand, depending each on his ability to meet the demand on as favourable terms as his neighbour. This is legitimate competition, and calls out the most energetic administration of affairs. Though it be a struggle, it can hardly be called a conflict. Each party has brought into combination the skill, labour and capital required in the production of their respective fabrics, and the contest between them is the natural result of a principle of general acceptance, that men strive to do the best they can for themselves. So far, the workmen and the capitalists are side by side in a common interest in the articles they produce.

The workmen and the capitalists will each desire for their fabric such a control in the market as will sustain the cost of production. The contest between them is not to enhance or reduce the price of the article, but for the ratio each shall receive of the product. It is obvious the market price will be regulated by the action of others, as well as their own. It will be seen that practically there is a peculiarity in the most usual demonstrations of this struggle, that does not hold in the general competitions of business. The fallacy of the struggle is in the attempt to disregard the laws of demand and supply; an effort that can only embarrass and tend to produce mischief. Here we have the parties, workmen and capitalists engaged in the production of the same article, and any antagonism that defeats negotiation is likely to prove injurious to both.

The rights of parties in this conflict are as readily discovered as in any other competition. The two have each his own rights. The workman has his skill and labour, and the capitalist his capital and administrative ability ; each party has equal right to make the most of his own that the market will afford. If capital is abundant, it must yield to the laws of trade and be content with a corresponding profit or interest. The same holds good with the workman; he must be controlled by the same laws of demand and supply. In so far as the workman has command of sufficient capital to provide for the instrumentality of his own production, no conflict in this respect can arise. Here it is seen how important it is that the workman have so much capital as will suffice to make his labour most productive. This position may be reached in many branches of industry by a young man who has the self-control to make the best of his situation. Such do their own work, and hold their own instruments, securing to themselves both the wages and profits of their production.

The importance of this question of conflict arises in the cases where large capital, beyond the ordinary means of individual workmen, is required to provide the outlay, and carry on current operations by the most economical process. It is not material in such case whether the capital be furnished by one or by the co-operation of several persons. The necessity of the case is, the fabric to be produced is of a nature that requires for its most economical production, a large outlay in lands, mills, machinery, raw stock and wages. These being provided, it is necessary workmen be

employed to manage the machinery, and thus bring out
the anticipated result in the production of the fabric.
Here are clearly two parties ; one would not produce
without the other. Each has his right of contract,
and a proper motive for securing such result as the
market may warrant.

The capitalist predicates his enterprise on the laws
of trade ; based on the ordinary estimates of his power to produce an article that will yield a suitable return
for his outlay. In this estimate he considers the
rate of wages he must pay, on the basis of the market
value of the labour he will require. This must be considered a sound method of proceeding. If the capitalist
is an experienced manufacturer, his estimates will be
more reliable than if he depend on the advice of an
expert he cannot fully know, and who may not thoroughly understand the details of the proposed work,
or he may have some interest not consistent with that
of the capitalist. In either case it is subject to contingencies that no sagacity may foresee ; a risk that
must be taken by the capitalist in all the larger classes
of production that engage the enterprise of men.

The outlay being made—the mills, machinery and
tools ready, the workmen enter on the work of operating
the mill, having made engagement on certain terms,
which, in view of the labour market, they regard as their

interest to accept, and the mill has gone into operation. By and by, as occasion happens, the workmen become dissatisfied with their wages or rate of pay. When they engaged they no doubt considered their agreement as the best method of finding a market for their skill and labour. So far as their engagement extended, they were bound in law and equity to fulfil and satisfy their contract, same as all men are bound by their contracts. On the other hand, there was the same right of the workmen to demand of the employer the full compliance of the contract on his part.

No doubt any one has the right on the completion of his contract to seek other engagement if desired. To this no one can object ; and if his workmen leave him, the capitalist must find others to supply their places. There are several causes that may properly induce a workman to leave his occupation in the establishment in which he had been engaged, and if his contract is fulfilled, no one has a right to complain, as it is clearly his right to obtain the best market he can find for his skill and labour. Nor is the case changed if all the workmen in the mill take the same course. They may do this on a question of wages, or in reference to some regulation of rules or method of business. Having completed their engagements, they are at liberty to leave the work and seek employment

where it promises to be more satisfactory to themselves.

Thus far, there is no proper controversy—each
party has exercised his legitimate right. But if the
workman has taken advantage of some peculiar circumstance whereby the employer is thrown into unusual embarrassment, then he is wrong, though he
may not have violated the letter of his engagement.
For instance, the employer may have made contracts
for his fabric that he would not have done had he
known of the intention of his workmen to leave him ;
and their act in this case would be regarded as an
effort to coerce him to do what would be under his
contract a losing business. This would be a moral
wrong on the part of the workmen, if they had given
no notice ; and though the owner may have no remedy, he will feel that he has not been fairly treated. A
further circumstance may influence this question : the
workman may consider the outlay in the mill will be
unprofitable, or a serious loss to the owner, unless it
be operated, and that he will prefer to run it on very
small or no profit, rather than have it idle. This may
bring the employer to consider if he has not been
mistaken in his enterprise. But this cannot be re-
called, and if it have any influence, it will probably be
to warn him against extension of his works, and oth-

ers from embarking in similar enterprise. If there was no remedy, the interest of both capital and labour would be injured by such controversy, as tending to arrest enterprise.

If, however, the capitalist has gone into the work with an intelligent understanding of the subject, he probably will not abandon his enterprise. If the workmen he had employed leave him, he will be compelled to look about the market, and if he has conducted his operations with discretion, will find others who will probably be very ready to fill their places. He will know the value of labour in the market rests on the same basis that controls the price of fabrics ; both equally depending on the one law of supply and demand ; and this law will not only be respected, but control, whatever any man may do or claim. It will therefore only be a question of time for a new set of men to be provided. This state of things will nevertheless be more or less a damage to the capitalist or owner of the mill, and tend to discourage enterprise in the production that may be fabricated. But there is no escape from this contingency. At times the workmen, in order to correct what they regard a wrong, resort to a strike as a remedy.

CHARACTERISTICS OF A STRIKE.

The strike, if general, will probably work an evil to
the workman in most cases, as the derangement of
business will usually be a damage to both parties. It
is productive of a suspension of both wages and
profits, that cannot be resumed until the difficulty is
adjusted. It is a condition of things that rarely happens, without imprudent proceedings on one side or the
other.

Unfavorably, or perhaps I may say unfortunately,
this is not the whole of what is usually termed a
strike. If it were, the evil to business would be far
less than contemplated by the striking or disbanded
workmen. It often, and most generally, happens the
disbanded workmen do all in their power to prevent
others from supplying their places This no doubt
arises largely from the fact that they do not well understand the laws of trade, or the laws of society, by which
individual rights can be maintained. The workmen
have a perfect right to say to others—the wages are too
low, or the rules unreasonable ; but any step of coercion,
by violence or intimidation, is a rebellion, not only
against the laws of trade, but also against the laws of
society. For one set of men to say to another, you
shall not work except on our terms, and so interfere

with the interest of the second and third parties (there are two parties wronged), is, especially to the obstructed workman, an oppressive tyranny. In so far as such measures are effectual, the workman is restrained of his legitimate right to sell his skill and labour on such terms as he regards his interest. It will readily be perceived, this produces a conflict with the rights and interest of society, who are not only entitled to their rights of labour, but also to the protection of their interest in all that relates to a free commercial activity in both capital and labour. Consequently the government here steps in, and restrains from all proceedings of violence or intimidation that disturb or infringe on the rights of others—jeopardize the peace of society, or in any way interfere with the legitimate working of commercial and political freedom. The laws of trade and of civilization are equally to be maintained against any such anarchy and oppression as would result from the tyrannical power by which one man, or one set of men, should be able to say to another—you shall not work, except as I dictate.

Working-men are generally in favour of freedom and the just rights of men. They revolt against the power that would deprive them of these, from whatever despotic source of authority it may come ; and certainly they should not exercise it against their fellow-work-men.

Strikes among working-men, of the kind referred to, are simply an effort to counteract the laws of trade ; and so is every device to secure an advantage by any sort of monopoly. In most cases they will be attended by loss, both to workmen and employer. No well-regulated industry ever allows a strike to succeed in its purpose. In view of any change in the market, intelligent business men will regulate the wages they pay on the basis of supply and demand ; and in view of any cause likely to produce dissatisfaction, will timely adjust their affairs to meet the circumstances that may indicate a change in the labour market. A strike may arise from a stringent or oppressive way of the employer; or the strike may arise from a demand of the workmen that is inconsistent with the condition of the market for labour and the pro-duct of their labour. Obviously the product is affected by the cost of the necessary labour.

After wages and regulations of work, there is an-other and very unreasonable cause for strikes—that one workman is paid higher wages than another in the same department. It is notorious, that some work-men are worth more than others on the same kind of work ; and it is not only unjust the superior workman should be deprived of the value of his labour, but equally unreasonable inferior workmen should be paid the same wages as the superior. A skilful workman who performs his work faithfully, will rarely have occasion to resort to any other means of redress for any dissatisfaction than to signify to some other establishment that he is ready to engage with them for his services; while a different sort of workman will aim to advance his position or wages by a strike.

There is doubtless another side to this question. The same motive of self-interest that leads to a strike among workmen, may, and no doubt does at times, induce employers to pursue a course towards their workmen that is more or less stringent and oppressive. Under such circumstances it is the right of the workmen to devise such measures as promise relief. It may be there is difficulty in doing this. Any difficulty will be increased by the dependence of the men on their wages for current subsistence. This should impress the importance of habits of economy as a means of independence. It is obvious if the workman be dependent, he may not be able, without suffering, to suspend work until he can find it with an employer who will be satisfactory. This calls attention to

Trades Unions

By which contributions are made for the support of workmen on a strike. In this, reliance is had on the disposition of the owner to yield, in order to avoid the loss he would incur from his unemployed mill. This can only succeed in cases where the owner has failed to correctly understand the laws of supply and demand in the labour market. It is impossible that work should go on, independent of this rule, for any considerable time. This is evident on the least reflection, as the ruin of the owner would be inevitable if the wages could not be sustained by the market value of the fabric produced. Contributions to the Union must be voluntary, and of course limited, and instances have occurred in which a strike has been continued for months, and with all the aid the Union could furnish, caused much suffering to the men out of employment.

In the course of my life I have known many and some very severe strikes among workmen, and have in no instance known one to succeed when a proper attention on the part of the employer was given to the law above stated. But if the employer has been unreasonable in respect to those laws, he may find it necessary to modify his practice. In such case, it is

very probable the strikers will gain their object, and the
owner realize a loss that naturally results from his
indiscreet management.   On the other hand, the discreet owner will allow his mill to be idle, rather than
run it at a loss for any considerable time.   The Union
referred to can only depend on voluntary contributions, and at best can afford but a scanty support even
for a moderate length of time.   It should be improved
by the contributing workmen, to cultivate those habits
of saving that may give substantial improvement to
their affairs, when no such draft is made on their
earnings.

There is obviously a direct loss to both parties,
in the operation of a strike ; and it is clearly the part
of wisdom to exercise every practicable measure to prevent it.   Each party has an interest in this.   To do it,
it is only necessary to fairly consider the situation or
circumstances that control.   Neither party can be justified in taking a position inconsistent with this.
Both capital and labour have respectively a right to
their earnings, and these must be referred to the laws
of trade, on the basis of existing markets ; a reference
that eventually must prevail, whatever course may be
pursued by these parties.

Difficulties sometimes arise from the varying circumstances of production, as when an establishment,

similar to others in its work, has a specialty in the production of certain articles, for which it is peculiarly adapted, or has the protection of a patent, that gives the control of the market. Under these circumstances the mill may pay a higher rate than the usual wages. Now the workmen in mills that do not have such advantage are very likely to take the one that has as a standard, and refuse to work unless at the same rate. The peculiar establishment may be able to employ only a small portion of the men who do this or analogous work, and consequently the larger portion can only obtain such wages as may be warranted in works of more general character, where the special advantages are not enjoyed. It may be the specialty cannot employ a fourth part of that class of workwen, and consequently three fourths will be able to earn only such wages as can be afforded on general work of that class. It is therefore unreasonable to insist on the same basis of wages as may be paid by the specialty. The product of the goods made must determine the wages. It is further to be observed, that in such cases the specialty usually obtains the best workmen for their class of work—men whose actual worth is above the average.

There can be no doubt this, as all other affairs of business, must be adjusted by the law of supply and demand. The sentiment, that labour is worth so much, or more or less, is without foundation. It is worth just what it will command in the market, same as any other commodity. There is no other philosophy than this. The benevolent idea that wages should be such as to yield a fair support, is necessarily indefinite, and has little or no application in the commerce of men. Business is one thing and charity another. Nor would the charitable view comport with the dignity of labour, or lead to any other than the pauper, or semi-pauper plan which no able-bodied American citizen should respect, or propose for his support. It is, moreover, totally unnecessary in this country, where every man has the right of labour, and the right to choose the kind he regards most for his interest in all the variety of labour that constitutes the instrumentality by which most, if not all the wealth or property of the country has been gathered. Let no man in a free country speak diminutively of the power of labour, but bear in mind, that most of our capitalists, large and small, began to gather, and continued to gather, by savings from their labour.

Why then should the workmen be dissatisfied with the capitalist? Consider the question on its real merits. Suppose, then, there were no men that accumulated capital ; from whence, then, would be found

the means to build mills, supply machinery, raw stock
and wages ? If there were none that acquired capital,
there would be none to provide these instruments,
by which labour finds its principal employment—its
absence from society would necessarily throw us back
to the primitive order of things, and both labour and
population would be greatly reduced. Even the handi-
craft arts would feel this, as well as the higher or
more complicated orders of occupation. There can
be no doubt the enterprise of capital is the main
feature that enlarges the field, and consequently the
demand for labour, and this increases its market
value. At the same time, the labourer has his share
of the benefits that flow from the more efficient and
economical production that arises from the instruments that capital is able to put into the hands of labour.

If the non-capitalist has neglected or lost his
opportunity to acquire capital by any want of education or self-control, he should be careful to see that
his son does not lose it.

No doubt there is an advantage in the ownership of capital or property sufficient to secure an
independent occupation; and this is the very reason
that induced the system of self-control, of industry and
frugality by which it has been acquired by the capitalist. There can be no just ground for complaint on

the part of those that did not acquire it. They preferred a course of indulgence that was incompatible with such result; and after the habit of using the earnings of all the powers they employed in various and unprofitable sources of present gratification, it is clearly unreasonable for them to complain of those who had the wisdom and prudence to control and so regulate their desires as to reach the enviable condition of the capitalist and other independent holders of property.

It is charged that the holders of property are sometimes oppressive. No doubt this is true, and the main reason may be found in the fact that so large a proportion of men are unwilling to exercise the self-control that is necessary to acquire property. If all were industrious and frugal, there would be very little of the dependence that gives capital undue power. Instead of concentrating, capital would be more diffused, more abundant, and interest and profits on funds would be reduced. Under existing circumstances the general charge of oppression is not well founded; for in most cases the labourer receives the full rate of wages the market will command, and is paid at short intervals out of the funds of the capitalist, before the latter can realize from the sale of his product, and often months in advance.

No just government will allow one citizen to oppress another, whoever that citizen be. The government takes no measures to require parties to engage in contract; that under law is one of the inalienable rights of men ; but after the contract is made, the government will see that its conditions are enforced. This is one of the great duties of government ; without which civilization could not exist. Take another branch in commercial affairs as an illustration of this principle :—A set of men undertake to control the market in the article of flour—they buy up all the flour they can reach, and set their own price on it, and none can interfere—they have so far exercised a legal power. But if some party in the community has flour not controlled by the forestallers, or monopolists, and offers the sale at lower rates, and the monopolists should endeavour to coerce him to hold his flour at the same rate the monopoly dictated—would any community submit to this? In such case all will say,—the government must interfere and prevent such tyranny. This is precisely analogous to the workman who seeks to coerce and obstruct his fellow-workman in the pursuit of his legitimate right to make such contract for his skill and labour as he regards his interest.

The labourer is free, and under no obligation to obey the decree of the union—the government will protect him. This is so obviously necessary to secure individual freedom and the just rights of men, that open coercion is not often practised. The proceedings therefore to enforce this kind of tyranny will be (as most usual) by threats, so made as to evade legal cognizance, by attacks on the person of the workman, under cover of darkness, on his way home, or in some position of unseen or defenceless condition. This is rebellion against society; and it is a humiliation to believe there are working-men in this free country that can be guilty of a proceeding which only befits those who seek darkness to hide their transactions, or that an honest workman will follow the wake of the criminal who preys on the rights of society, by seeking the obscurity of night to hide his transactions, and all in an effort to counteract the free action of the laws on which industry and society rest. If such proceedings could succeed, the foundation of social order would be broken, and anarchy and confusion reign. No stable basis would remain on which industry could rest ; no inducements to acquire its instruments, and industry would necessarily be prostrated and civilization arrested.

The safety of order and society rests on the fact that there are several classes in society that would oppose such result. First, the capitalist—Second, men of independent competence in property—Third, those who practice industry and economy, with a view to reach one of the two preceding classes. All these, and others that might be mentioned, are too much interested in maintaining the order of civilized society to allow the anarchy, confusion and tyranny that would break up the law of free commercial activity, and lead us back to barbarism—where no law would protect the weak, and no enterprise enlarge the basis of productive industry. Probably the coercing Trades Unions or strikers do not see this tendency; for I am sure if they did a large proportion of them would hesitate to proceed on a course so fraught with danger to every interest connected with our civilization, which to an American working-man should be invaluable.

When men are oppressed by arbitrary and despotic government, we can see some excuse for the violent men who hope to gain, though it may be through confusion and anarchy; but even under such circumstances their success is usually far below, if in any considerable degree they reach, their expectations.

If in any respect men desire to be free, they must be able to govern themselves. Their own passions must be brought into subjection to reason and sense; and they must learn to extend the same freedom to others they seek and claim for themselves. In short, to cultivate a love and respect for the right—the only freedom worth having—in truth there is no other. The freedom men sometimes claim of doing as they please, and at the same time of compelling others to do as they dictate, is the oppressive tyranny of a despot, whoever claims it ; and should be abhorred by every American working-man who raises his hand and voice in support of the right and dignity of labour.

In this country labour is free to command the market, same as any commodity, however produced. No one is privileged (except in so far as that fallacy called protection to labour has prevailed) ; even capital is, in the main, only a product of labour, beginning with small or no material means, and there is no proper reason why all (barring exceptional cases) should not be capitalists, or at least reach to a comfortable degree of independence. Absolute independence is not supposed, for no such case exists. We are all, more or less, in various ways dependent on our fellows ; but the independence which gives the instruments of labour, and the power of our situation to command a supply of our reasonable wants, is what is intended.

Perhaps it may be a delicate matter to discuss the cause of so great disparity as we find to exist in the condition of men. But the wound can only be cured by a thorough probing. The question that first

presents itself for consideration is—why is it that
men starting on the same platform, reach such
different results ? Some attaining conditions of
comfort and affluence, while others struggle through
life, barely securing a scanty subsistence ? There
must be cause for this. Doubtless the variety in
natural ability, and the opportunities of life, are causes
of various degrees of success. But these only account
for the degrees in which some obtain a competence
and others large wealth. They leave a large class of
dependent men. How shall their condition be
accounted for ? Does it not result from ignorance,
uncontrolled appetite and passion, tending inevitably
to the improvidence that destroys all prospect of
saving even the instruments of their simplest occupation ? Is there no remedy ? I believe there is. Education has shown its power for this, in the large numbers that have succeeded, and have given strength to
our civilization by which we have established Institutional law, and the order of social being : I therefore
look to education—mental, moral and religious—as the
hope of reducing this class, until there shall be none
left, save such as by natural imbecility are incompetent to reach a condition of independence. Mental
education is of prime value; but moral and religious is
necessary to cultivate respect for the rights of others,

indispensable for a just and free government, and for the subjugation of the appetites and passions to their useful and proper purposes of life.

A Christian community, well instructed in the cardinal principles of their religion, will cultivate industry and frugality, and steadily improve in their material as well as their moral well-being. This is corroborated by the experience of those Christian communities that have observed and practised the duties and principles of the religion introduced into the world by Jesus Christ. Such people are not found in the seats of dissipation, wasting their time and means in idle conviviality. It is the hope of the friends of a true education, that its influence will subdue ignorance and increase the power of self-control, and so lead to the industry, prudence and economy that is productive of material and moral well-being. It certainly must be relied on as one at least of the great pillars that sustain the social fabric, and tend to the diminution of the dependent class of men.

This is a great thing to hope and work for. The development of a true education would greatly increase the product of skill, labour and capital, and all men be better sheltered, fed and clothed ; and be surrounded with the means of mental, moral and religious culture, greatly adding to the individual and social happiness of men.

The wages is not the whole of "Trades Unions." The " Unions " extend their operations to the rules and manner of work, in such a way as to diminish the quantity that may be done in regard to the instruments that shall be used, and also as to the locality from whence materials may be had.

Professor Cairnes has quoted from Mr. Thornton (the latter an advocate for measures of amelioration to the labourer) some of the rules of the " Union." On page 258, " Political Economy," he quotes : " At Manchester this combination is particularly effective, preventing any brick made beyond a radius of four miles from entering the city." . . . . " The vagaries of the Lancashire brickmakers are fairly paralleled by the masons of the same country." . . . . " The York- shire masons, however, will not allow Yorkshire stone to be brought into their district if worked on more than one side. All the rest of the working,—the edge- ing and jointing,—they insist in doing themselves, though they thereby add thirty-five per cent to its price." . . . . " A master mason at Ashton obtained some stone ready polished." . . . . " His men, how- ever, in obedience to the rules of the club, refused to fix it until the polished part had been defaced and they had polished it again by hand, though not so well as at first." . . . . " The Manchester bricklayers ' association have a rule providing that any man found running, or working beyond a regular speed, shall be fined," &c., " as also shall be any man working short-handed, without man for man." . . . . "During the building of the Manchester law court, the bricklayers' labourers struck because they were desired to wheel brick instead of carrying them on their shoulders." More might be quoted from the rules of the " Union," but the above is sufficient to show the policy of certain working-men in this matter of " Union."

The preceding are from English " Unions." I do not know if American Unions go to the same extent, but they do not discard the features of the English Unions, and in some respects adopt them.

American working-men have made considerable effort to obtain the enactment of laws regulating the time of a day's work. Nothing has been better settled by the experience of mankind, than that government interference with the business affairs of men is always bad, and especially so for labouring men. Except in the case of children, in order to protect them from the cupidity of their guardians and employers, no government interference has proved a benefit to the labourer, beyond that of protecting him in his just rights of labour and enterprise.

Our working-men have petitioned government to

prevent the employment of convict labour, where it may be supposed to come in competition with the industries of society. From the necessities of their condition the convicts, if employed at all advantageously, their work must be such as can be done in a shop. If they make hats, the hatter complains ; if they make cabinet ware, then the cabinetmaker complains ; if shoes, the shoemaker complains, and so of every trade that must work in a shop. Listening to these petitions from various classes of citizens, the Legislature of the State of New York authorized measures to employ the convicts on mining works, a kind very unsuitable for convicts—all which has proved very unprofitable to the State. The obvious purpose of the State, in employing convicts in the production of useful commodities, is to make them earn their subsistence, and at the same time improve their habits of industry. If the convict cannot be so employed as to earn his subsistence, he must be supported at public expense, by taxation on all classes of society. The main question is, shall this labour be annihilated ? If this be answered in the affirmative, then certainly so much labour of the country must be lost. So far as this could prevail, its influence on the cost of production would be to make goods dearer. In other words, to diminish the products of industry. If these convicts had not been criminals, their labour would probably have been more formidable as competitors in the labour market, than it is in their condition of convicts. If in this matter the theory of the working-men is correct, then it is their interest the number of convicts be increased, and so take out of the ranks of industry the largest number the State may be able to support in idleness or unproductive labour. This would be absurd, but it is the logical conclusion of their theory.

It is apparent the undisguised policy of "Trades Unions" is to impair the results, or to make labour as impotent as possible. If then there be any such thing as a "wages fund," their policy leads to its destruction as rapidly as possible. They probably do not see the logical results of their rules and regulations. If they refuse the use of a wheelbarrow, and compel bricks to be carried by hand, they cannot be expected to check their operations until the use of all agents in transportation is discontinued, and all burdens borne on the shoulders of men ; and instead of horses, the plough must be drawn by gangs of men—the natural agents, as steam and water must be laid aside and the machinery (if any) be propelled by manual labour. Such a result it is impossible to reach, though it is the logical conclusion from the premises advocated by "Trades Unions."

7

Look carefully at the principles of " Trades Union." If they are correct, then certainly any invention or improvement that renders labour more effective is an impediment, and consequently an injury to the working-man—all natural agents that reduce manual labour should be discarded, and the greatest possible amount of manual labour should be bestowed on any fabric required for the use of men. Can any one suppose this would benefit labour? If it could, then the opinion of mankind has been greatly at fault, and barbarism is to be preferred to civilization ; or to depend for sustenance on the chase and the gathering of fish and natural fruit, is better for labouring men than the well-ordered industries of civilization.

Trades Unions on Apprenticeship.

The policy of Trades Unions in regard to apprenticeship is designed to restrict the number in any branch of mechanics. The manifest object of this is to limit the number, in order to increase the rate of wages. That is, that there be the least number of men in any branch that may suffice to command the highest rate of wages the industry may afford to pay. It is manifest this course will tend to reduce the amount of work in any industry, and increase the cost of what may be done, destroying the benefit of commercial freedom, and so increasing the cost of goods to the community. If it could be made to apply to all industries, the workman in one department would be compelled to pay for the goods he needed from the other departments as much advance as he gained in his own, and he could obtain no benefit from this artificial obstruction. If the workman looks at this thing in its true light, he will see, that in order to benefit himself, all goods except his own product should be free, so that while he obtains favour no other goods that he needs should be restricted to this narrow monopolizing system.

The policy of the Union is, that no mechanic in the association is allowed to take an apprentice, except as may be directed by the Union. It may be the interest of some member of the Union to employ an apprentice, and a candidate may be in waiting for such employment. But if the Union say no, these parties are prohibited from exercising a natural right.

No man can properly be compelled to take an apprentice, for this is a matter he must consider in view of his own interest. It is quite necessary the candidate present adequate inducement. This is all a matter of business freedom, and in every rational view should be regarded as conclusively settling the action of the parties. Now, the Union steps in and says to the mechanic, there are enough now in your trade, and according to the rules of the Union, you cannot take another. Here the just rights of two parties are broken down by a monopoly, that so far as it goes, destroys commercial freedom. Nor are these injured parties the only interest involved in this transaction of the Union ; for it is manifest, the rights of the public are trampled upon, in a most despotic manner. If freedom is worth anything to the working-man, he should consider, if this principle of the Union is not an arbitrary means for its destruction. Certainly no right can be more important to the individual and to society, than that which leaves every man free to make such contract for his services as he regards his interest. No man in a free country can question this position as the basis of commercial freedom.

To this the Unionist says, No, you shall enter no engagement except at our dictation. How does this differ from the flour, or any other arbitrary monopoly, that aims to break down the barriers of commercial freedom, and in its place establish a despotic rule, which goes directly to the subversion of civil liberty, breaking down the benign principle that is the only security for the rights of man, and the free activity of industrial economy.

The whole theory will be discarded by intelligent working-men, as inconsistent with their happiness, and a manly regard for the power and dignity of un-shackled labour. The system of "Trades Union" fails to perceive the true method by which the working-man has been, and will be, elevated to the character and benefits he may reach by a manly exercise of his powers of production. If, therefore, he allow himself to slide into the dependent class, it will be for the reason, that he has failed to properly improve his powers.

Methods have been proposed by which, in some way, it is aimed to show how labour and capital may be combined to effect a more equitable ratio between wages and profits. I propose to consider some of these propositions.

COMMUNITY PLAN.

This has been followed in several instances, and in some with great perseverance and well-intended purpose to improve the advantages of the labourers. So far as I understand this method, the community is an association, composed of a body of men and women, who place themselves under a mutual association, in which their labour and their property becomes a common stock. They labour in common, and have a common support out of the aggregate product of their labour

and capital.   In these communities all are professedly
on equal terms, under the regulations of the association.   Here the labour is supposed to be more efficient,
and the supplies had on better terms or more cheaply;
and as a consequence, the material wants of the association better supplied, than they could be by individual enterprise and labour.

These communities have been organized and maintained for considerable time, and their characteristics
pretty fairly developed.   In some cases they have been
placed on the basis of some religious principle, and in
others resting solely on the basis of material interest.
Some prohibit sexual intercourse, and by this means
avoid the care and expense of raising children.   Others
allow, and are supposed to practice, promiscuous sexual
commerce, which brings them into the category of the
brothel.   In both these cases they are at war with the
institution of the family, as established by the Creator;
thus breaking up the original order, and sapping the
foundation of the marriage institution, which most
eminently sustains public and private virtue.

It is believed such communities, by their united
skill and industry, produce many useful articles, at a
moderate cost, and sustain their material support in
a good degree of abundance.   They move along in
routine on the orders, and depend on the care and

providence of their ruling elders. No brilliancy of mind is expected in these associations. We do not expect to see them produce a Pallissy, a Watt, an Arkwright, a Whitney, a Fulton, a Morse, or any of similar character who form the host of distinguished men, who by their individual skill and perseverance have wrought out and brought into operation those vast improvements in the arts that minister to the wants of men, and have given better food, clothing and shelter to the civilized world.

It was stated the community hold themselves as all on a footing of equality. In this respect it is to be observed, the sentiment is not practically carried out. Every kind of government, even a community or association, must have its order. Hence, certain elders are placed in charge of affairs, and on their capacity, and specially on their executive ability and fidelity, the success of the community will depend. Probably individuals may offer counsel, but the head must rule or affairs would soon work badly. It is a democracy, with a head that rules the body. A body of men who, from whatever motive, are willing to give up their individuality, and trust for the direction of their industry and the supply of their wants to the providence of one or more of their number who directs their work and does their thinking for them, is not likely to rebel against authority, nor can it be expected they will advance in the culture and refinements of civilization. Excepting the ruling members, it is almost on a dead level of monotony.

An important fact in relation to the community is, that comparatively a small number of men are willing to bury their personality in a community of this kind. From the very characteristics of the human mind, it cannot be expected that any who feel the dignity of their personality, will consent to such an absorption, and thus bury their individuality in the community. For this reason, it cannot be expected (except for those who rule) the community will obtain recruits except from the class of weak-minded persons who have not the manliness to maintain their independence. This is no doubt the main reason why they have made so little progress in the world. It certainly does not promise essential amelioration in the question of capital and labour. The system necessarily leaves out of view the principle of personal independence that nerves the mind to vigorous effort, and which has achieved the great works of civilization.

GOVERNMENT AID TO LABOR.

I propose but few remarks under this head. The thing is so absurd in any economic view, that it would not be noticed, except for some recent claim on the aid of government to assist labour. The French made an experiment of this kind shortly after the revolution of 1848. What were known then as the comunists, claimed it as a duty of government to provide work for the people. This folly was listened to, and led to the establishment by government of shops for the fabrication of goods. It did not require much time to demonstrate this to be not only absurd, but ruinous to the government. Those shops, except so far as they were for military purposes, have been, as I understand, abandoned, and the idea of the communists has only been partially maintained in the way of municipal and other public works, which have been sufficiently impressive in the onerous taxes that follow in the wake of every attempt of government to do what should be done, and can much better be done, by individual enterprise.

Not long since a convention of working-men met at the city of Pittsburgh. On that occasion they set forth a project for the government to furnish funds at a low rate of interest, to miners and others, as a capital that would enable them to dispense with the aid of banks, and so carry on industrial enterprise without dependence on capitalists. Their idea, probably had its origin in the supposition the government had funds, and that it was its duty to aid the working class of men. Whereas, the fact is, the government has got no money or resources, except in taxes; and if it furnish funds to one class of men, it can only do so by taxing all classes. The impolicy, the injustice of this, did not suggest itself to the convention. Such propositions are no credit to the intelligence of working-men, who should have at least the sagacity to see their absurdity. It was a chimerical proposition, and would not be worthy of notice, except that it was brought forward as a measure to adjust the question of capital and labour. The working-men should know that governments, when they have undertaken to provide for them, have done more for their degradation than for their improvement, and that the only real service the government can do for working-men, is to maintain their rights as freemen, and thus secure to them the full product of their skill, labour and enterprise in all the range of productive labour. Men are prone to forget the great truth that it is only as individuals a community can properly prosper. This is the basis and strength of our civilization, and the hope of its progress.

Co-Operative Industry.

By this it is understood that labour and capital shall be associated, so that both shall be represented by the same parties. That is, working-men unite their means in order to provide the capital that may be necessary for the economical production of the goods they propose to fabricate. The plan has many advocates, and to some extent has been put in practice. The idea is certainly a very plausible one, and to the minds of many persons, offers the best solution of the question of labour and capital. Some remarks have been made on this problem, and it is now proposed to examine it in more detail.

In all the industries that admit, it is obviously the best method for the workman to hold in his own right so much capital as is needed to conduct his work most economically. It is favourable that there are many industries requiring but a moderate amount of capital in funds to conduct them ; not more than any industrious and prudent man may acquire by his own savings in a few years. After this comes a class of industries that may require the partnership of two or three in order that their joint means may be sufficient. So far there is no difficulty that is not common to all business, in settling the labour question.

A firm or partnership of two or three persons may be regarded in a limited degree as a co-operative company. But this is not what is usually understood by co-operative industry. The latter looks to a more extensive association, designed to compass a larger business, and may include twenty to one hundred or more persons. With even ten persons in such an association, it is difficult to see how such a party could be better organized than as a

JOINT–STOCK CORPORATION.

In any other way it would be very inconvenient, if not impracticable, to conduct their business. Under an act of incorporation the association could establish rules of business, and direct the general method of operation, and choose their executive managers. If, as I suppose, there is no better way, then co-operative industry becomes corporate industry, and the association is a corporation. In this case each member would be a stockholder according to the proportion of funds he contributed. This seems the most simple plan of conducting any association designed for the larger class of industries, where large capital, together with labour, must be united to effect the most economical production of goods. This method is quite practicable, as in most of the States laws provide for and authorize the formation of such corporations for manufacturing and mining purposes. The field is open to all working-men.

The question naturally occurs, why has it not been more availed of by working-men? The way is certainly open and free. There must be some reason why they have not improved it. In reference to this, I remark. In some kinds of production there is a comparatively small proportion of skilled labour. To a large extent it is the labour of common labourers, females and minors, who are not possessed of the funds required, nor skilled in the executive duties required to manage large works. If such works are to be conducted, there must of necessity be some, if not the principal part, of the funds obtained from those who are not working people. Not to embarrass this discussion, I shall look at the productions that mostly demand skilled labour.

It is well known there are excellent workmen who can manage well their own work, but have very little of the executive skill necessary to lay out and plan work for a shop or even a department of a shop. If such as these, as most probable, compose a portion of the association, they must be subject to the manager of the shop, or the foreman in their department of work. There should be no difficulty in this, as the

manager is supposed to understand what is best to be
done by each member. To submit to this rule it is
necessary there be confidence in the skill and fidelity
of the executive head; and such self-control on the
part of the workman as will induce him to yield his
own opinion, if in conflict with the manager or foreman. Now the company, and the original authority
are the workmen themselves, and if these have not
the culture of self-restraint, that will readily yield to
the direction of those empowered to control affairs,
they will soon lose the benefit of harmonious action.
It is impossible to regulate a large company of men
so as to work with economy unless there be rules and
authority to enforce the rules. Does this present a
difficulty to co-operation ? Every workman that enters
such an organization should carefully consider if he
is ready to submit his judgment to that of another
workman, who stands on the same corporate plane
with himself, and has no other authority than that
given by himself and associates. If the workmen have
not the culture to yield to this discipline, they are not
prepared for co-operative industry.

Let us see how a moderate case would work—say
one that will furnish work for twenty skilled labourers.
We have first to examine the question of funds required
for the land, mill or shop, mechanical power, machin-

ery and tools. For such an industry these could not
be estimated at less than thirty thousand dollars.
This may vary according to the production contemplated. To the outlay so far made there must be added
funds necessary for the purchase of raw stock, the
maintenance of the men during the reduction to the
finished fabric, and the credit that will probably be
required after the sale of the goods. These cannot
prudently be estimated at less than the first outlay,
namely, thirty thousand dollars. Total capital sixty
thousand dollars, or an average of three thousand
dollars for each man. It could hardly be expected
that twenty men for any specific industry would each
be able to furnish the three thousand dollars, nor
would it be necessary, as in a joint-stock corporation
each would furnish what he could, making the aggregate capital required.

The men should be so organized that each should
be paid for his work according to its value, and the
profits go to each according to his share in stock. It
cannot be doubted there would be some difficulty in
finding twenty men, in any one industry, who would
furnish the amount required. Men who had conducted
their affairs so prudently as to have three thousand
dollars at command, for a specific investment, would
very likely hesitate in so far putting it in the control

of a co-operate association as to lose its individual function.   It may be presumed there are cases where the men and the funds could be obtained for such an enterprise as contemplated, and on this supposition I proceed.

The company formed and the funds provided, and the men are supposed to be well skilled in the work proposed, the next thing will be the election of managers who are to supervise and conduct their operations.   This, of course, will be by the votes of the members.   The managers appoint a superintendent who is to conduct the operations of the work and supervise its general affairs.   It should be expected one of the company would fill this station.

A treasurer will be required to keep the books and manage the finances.   It might happen that some member of the association would be qualified for this duty; but this is doubtful.   A company of twenty skilled men, with the aid of mechanical power and machinery, would most probably have yearly transactions, in materials, wages and product, to the amount of one hundred thousand dollars, more or less, according to the character of the fabric they produced.   To conduct this branch properly will require a treasurer of considerable capacity, industry and integrity; and if this department is not properly conducted, the corporation will be likely to fail. The treasurer is an important officer in any joint-stock operation, and great care should be exercised in his selection, and in frequent examination of the books and finances. The association will have need of commercial experience, especially if the raw material is obtained and the product sold for distribution at distant points. To as great extent as the circumstances may permit, as for purchases and sales near by, or that may be conducted by letters, the treasurer may manage the general commercial business. If the industry is in a great measure a specialty, and distributed at prominent commercial centres, this department will be simplified. But if it be necessary to distribute mostly to consumers, a commercial agent may and most probably will be required. In the latter case, the success of the institution would depend very much on the agent. These general matters are necessarily involved in all large productions, and in the wisdom exercised in their management largely depends the success of the enterprise.

In view of my own experience, the most proper basis for an institution of this kind is, to pay all members, by stipulated wages, the same as they would pay a man not belonging to the company. If they were all equally efficient workmen, they would equitably be entitled to the same rate of pay. But this is not

8

probable ; some men will be more skilful, or better workmen than others, and so far as they work for day wages, will be entitled to a higher rate. The regular compensation of the men, either by piece or wages, is best, in order that each have the benefit of proper remuneration for his own labour. Any profit on the capital stock may then be divided to each according to his interest in the same, or it may be deferred for the purpose of strengthening the finances of the association as may appear desirable. The latter course is particularly advisable, rather than to depend on loans for current means.

In forming an association of this kind, it will not be safe to predicate on the supposition, that eveay man will do his duty freely. Though it must be admitted as probable, that the class of men who so prudently managed their affairs as to have the funds necessary for such an institution, will be very likely to see the propriety of conforming faithfully to regulations which they appreciate as proper for success, and which they have aided to establish. But the men do not so fully know each other as to warrant the adoption of this supposition. In all probability there will be necessity for more or less sifting out, and this can best be done by establishing a thorough system of business. A thoroughly able and good workman is most likely to be satisfied with sound business regulations. Though it is claimed that "all men are created equal," this must be regarded only as to equality of natural right. It would be a useless task to demonstrate that in many respects men are not equal, either by creation or training; and it is not to be supposed any twenty men, who may agree to go into an organization of associated labour, will be equally efficient and faithful.

Some will have less physical power, though of good skill. These may do their work well, but have not the same endurance, and consequently not the same power that occasion may require for special effort. It would also be remarkable in such an organization as proposed, if it should not turn out that some of them were inclined to idle their time, and be more fond of talk than of work. It should be kept in mind, it is the moral in the workman, no less than in the soldier, that gives energy to his operations. If he has not the nerve to resist the inclination, or the temptation to engage in telling or hearing strange and improbable stories, he will hardly live up to the wholesome rules of a well-established shop or mill. The above is a mere allusion to practical matters, that must be considered by any association for systematic labour, if they expect success. Consequently there must be a method, and power for correction when the necessity arises. This will not be difficult, if the majority is decidedly in favour of sound rules and their efficient enforcement.

To correct the inequalities of workmen, from whatever cause of deficiency, the practice of paying by the piece, rather than by day wages, has very generally come into use where the work admits. This gives the workman the benefit of any superiority he may have in skill or industry, and is the most ready method of adjusting the compensation. It does not dispense with rules, or the supervision of the foreman, who is required to inspect the quality of the work, and see that it is not improperly performed as to quality or progress. So far as work can be done by the piece, the mill or shop will be more productive.

In view of the importance, and indeed of the necessity of success, there must be supervision, and the conduct of all work and affairs be subject to a thorough administration under sound business rules. No man is to be shielded from the strict application of the rules of business, on the ground of his being a partner. Whatever be the intelligence of the men, their enterprise can only be a success through the systematic and efficient administration of an executive head. Even a body of twenty men can in no other way operate in the concert necessary to success.

No doubt there are industries that may be conducted economically with a less amount of funds and men than above stated ; but this is stated as a moderate one, in which labour and capital could be favourably combined for economical production, though much smaller than many branches require. If cooperative labour shall prove generally successful, it is probable there will be a greater subdivision in production. That is, the works that now produce several articles would be taken in parts, and so several companies may divide up and each become more specific in their productions. In former days, it was common for one establishment to spin the yarn, leaving the weaving to another, and the dying and dressing to still other parties. In the manufacture of steam engines, the boilers were made at one shop and the engine proper at another. In the manufacture of tools, machinery and the implements of agriculture, the production may be divided, and one company or firm produce one and another a different class. Every skilled workman will see how production may be divided, and still leave the work complete.

Though there seems no practical difficulties in making such divisions as above suggested, and others not necessary to particularize, it must be observed, that for some reason there is a tendency for similar industries to run into combination, and result in large mills or shops.   Of course these require larger executive ability in the power to systemize and arrange work for several departments.   Certain it is, that combination has of late years increased, and mills that did one branch only, now do several.   The presumption is, there are advantages in the larger works that have produced this change.   It is therefore important in establishing a mill for any division or branch of the work of a large establishment, that great caution be exercised in view of the competition that may be expected from the large mill.   No doubt a small establishment, under a company of industrious, skilful and prudent men, would have advantages peculiar to a small establishment ; and these may in many cases outweigh those of the large mill.

To this plan of co-operative labour there can be no objection.   The laws authorizing such associations have been for years on the statute books of most of the States of this Union.   Corporations in numerous cases have been formed under them.   A very large, if not the principal amount of the capital employed in the production of fabrics, has been organized in this way, for the class of larger industries.

It is not unusual for towns and villages to organize in corporations for manufacturing purposes ;

these not solely with a view to direct profit from the works, but to increase the industry and business of the town. In doing this, the requisite capital is often obtained with difficulty, and the result is more a public spirit for the improvement anticipated in the general business of the town, than any certain view of the profits that are expected from the enterprise itself. In such cases the workmen can take as much of the capital stock as they desire or can pay for. After the mill is erected and goes into operation, the workmen find employment, and will have opportunity to purchase shares of stock, most probably at easy rates, and so combine their skill and industry with their capital. It would not be necessary for them to take up the stock at once, or even the principal part, as they could purchase from time to time, according as they saved from their wages, and so steadily increase their ownership until they should be able to control the corporation. This opens a very easy method for a union of labour and capital—the organization perfected, the workmen may go forward systematically to acquire the stock capital, as they obtain means, and eventually become the owners of the mill. If they have ambition to combine labour and capital, this seems a very favourable way to secure their object. If much is anticipated from the union of labour and capital, hardly a more favourable opportunity could be expected.

Though the method above described appears a very favourable one for the co-operation of labour and capital, it does not appear that it has been adopted to any great extent by working-men. There must be some cause for this, and they should investigate and determine the reason.

PARTNERSHIP CORPORATION.

By this is meant a corporation by joint-stock, to raise the necessary funds. These funds may be subscribed by both working-men and by those having funds which they put into the corporation for the profit they expect from the enterprise. Not necessary that all, or even any of the workmen subscribe to the funds, or be at all known in the organization of the institution. The method contemplates that workmen are to be employed at such rate of compensation as may be agreed on, and to be regularly paid as in other works of the kind to be done. After paying all expenses, then, from the net profit that may remain, a certain rate of interest or dividend is to be paid on the capital stock, or carried to the credit of the stockholders, as compensation for the use of their funds ; and out of any balance of profit that may remain after paying the interest provided to be paid to the stock-holders, a certain rate of this balance shall be paid to the workmen that have been in regular service (barring any unavoidable detention from work) for the year or half year as the case may be, according to the amount of wages or pay received by each workman during the term provided for. This, it will be noticed, provides a certain percentage of the balance, after the first dividend of specific interest is paid on the stock. Now, if the rate of this distribution to the workmen be, say fifty per cent of the said balance, then the remaining fifty per cent of said balance will be divided as a further dividend to the stockholders on their stock capital. It will readily occur, that if nothing should remain after paying wages and other expenses, the stockholders would receive nothing for their capital.

The main feature of the plan is, that it provides a contingent benefit to the workmen out of the earnings of the mill after he has been paid his regular earnings. This can only be justified by the consideration that under this inducement the workmen will be more steady, prudent and diligent in conducting their work, and in the care of tools and materials. Under the circumstances most likely to exist in forming such a partnership, it is probable this would be more or less realized ; for only a steady class of men would be selected, or remain so long in the work as to be entitled to receive any percentage of the balance of profits. It is very probable this plan may work favourably, if the ratio of profits can be made satisfactory to both parties. It should exclude any workmen occasionally, or for a short time employed.

In regard to this partnership, it is necessary to consider how the capitalist will view it. His first observation will be—"Who is to secure me against the loss that may result ? no one can give me a guaranty. The workmen in any event must first be paid, and also all other current expenses, before I receive anything. It is obvious my funds must take the hazard of the enterprise, and unless it afford a profit, I get nothing. If I am only to receive the interest my funds would command on loan, there seems no object for me to take the risk. If successful beyond the rate of interest proposed, I must divide with those who have taken no risk, and have had the benefit of occupation. In taking the risk I may lose all ; it is therefore reasonable that I should have the benefit, if it occur, of corresponding profits ; which the plan reduces by in part giving it to those who have taken no risk at all."

The above position of the capitalist cannot be controverted, and he only finds the reason to induce him to this partnership, as before stated, namely—The superior productiveness of the work that may be expected from the ulterior interest the men have in the property of the establishment. No doubt there is force in this reason, especially when adopted for works that require mainly skilled labour. The capitalist must look upon it as a matter of business, and consider if it be probable this plan will secure that extra degree of diligence and care that will be equivalent to the extra compensation provided for. The method appears more promising as a means of harmonizing the conflict of labour and capital than any other I know of, after that of the corporation in which the workmen have their own capital, and so secure both wages and profits.

To the working-men it has the benefit of combining their interests under the management of men of more experience in financial and commercial affairs than they are likely to possess themselves, and at the same time affords them the opportunity, as they gather money from their savings, to purchase shares, and hold the stock capital, and so far become effectually and thoroughly co-operatives in labour and capital.

The plan provides, first, that the workmen are to be paid regular wages, and the interest to the stockholders paid out of net profits to a certain rate ; and second, the workman to be paid a certain rate out of any balance that may remain of net profit. If judiciously and satisfactorily arranged as to the rates to be divided, and guarded against incompetent or idle workmen, it appears a promising method of adjusting the question of capital and labour, in a way that will make both more productive. The danger is, that difficulty would sometimes arise in dismissing workmen who may have failed to satisfy the rules of the establishment. It will require a firm, upright and intelligent superintendent to do this duty, and if not wisely done, the institution will probably decline. The main feature of this plan, namely, the inducement it offers for men to do the best in their power to make the enterprise a success, is very important. In arranging wages and profits, a basis should be taken of moderate rates—depending for the more full compensation for both labour and capital out of the ultimate profits. Now it may be observed, no human affairs are infallible, and we can only depend on such organizations and management as wisdom and experience may dictate, and then do the best we can to improve and make them useful.

Remarks on the Preceding.

All combinations are subject to objections as to the economy of their operations. The individual who has his own capital and labour, will conduct his affairs, other things being equal, with more energy and careful thought than any corporation.   In his business operations there is no adverse counsel nor interest, nor unfaithful associate to mar his success.   So far as the individual, by his own labour and capital, can compass in an economical method the production of his goods, it is the best plan.   Next to this, there may be a partnership or firm, composed of two or three persons, for the purpose of uniting their capital and labour in a production requiring larger means than either may alone be able to furnish.

The next best source, especially for a young man whose occupation requires considerable capital, is an admission as a partner in an established industry. The advantages of this are obviously important, and may often be availed of by the young man who has obtained a good character for skill, industry and fidelity in his occupation.

Among the industries of life there is a large number, as before noticed, that may be pursued by the skilful workman with no more capital than an industrious and prudent young man may acquire in a few years, or that may be acquired by two or three to enable them to operate as a joint firm.   With prudent management they have in many cases founded important establishments; these have grown from comparatively small beginnings—enlarged from profits until they became extensive agents in production. Such frequently draw in to their aid and partnership younger men of their own vocation. Small beginnings have grown by this process, from the industry and perseverance of the men, to very large works.

In the several methods above named, of what may be called individual industries, there is no conflict between labour and capital; and as these embrace a very large portion of the industries of life, they present an important field for men who prefer an independent condition in the management of their own industry. It will be noticed these embrace whatever industry can be conducted with the capital of the workmen. But when these grow as before noticed, they more or less become employers of other workmen, and also involve to this extent the question of struggle between capital and labour.

It is not worth while to notice further the community plan. So far it has made but little progress, and if it could succeed to general adoption, it would destroy our civilization—uproot the principle of individuality, and thus break down the great stimulus to human progress, in all that elevates and refines society.

The plan of government management, by what is understood as the paternal method, is entirely irreconcilable with the principles of civil liberty, and will not be tolerated by any intelligent working-men who respect their rights and independence as freemen. No man of intelligence who does not desire our institutions to degenerate into despotism, will favour this method of adjusting the labour question. Far better for each man to stand on the free right to his own labour.

In the co-operative plan, which is understood to be the union of labour and capital, of such a number of workmen as may be necessary to provide the funds for any production they may contemplate, the work, if the plan is strictly carried out, should be done only by the partners who have furnished the capital. It is only to this extent the method meets the case of reconciliation between labour and capital. If the organization be by a joint-stock corporation, which appears to me the best method of association, then there would be no difficulty, if occasion required to employ outside workmen, at the market rate of wages, or as may be agreed on. To this plan I see no objection, and so far as it combined labour and capital, it would dispose of the labour question. It certainly has a very promising look, and may come into general use for the larger class of industries. But it must be observed that thus far it has made little progress ; suggesting difficulties in the way that have not been overcome, and in the present aspect does not promise to settle this question, until these difficulties are removed.

The plan of " partnership corporation " proposes the workmen have an interest in the ultimate profits of the institution, though they have no interest in the funds. For industries that require funds beyond the resources of the workmen, it presents a favourable prospect. If it be arranged on an equitable basis as to wages and profits, the workman may have the benefit of co-operation to the full extent of his means. He has, first, the benefit of wages for his work, with a contingent interest in the profits. He also has the benefit of so much of the capital stock as he may have funds to subscribe on the organization of the corporation ; with the opportunity of adding to his stock interest by the purchase of shares, as he obtains savings from his industries. He will very probably be able to purchase shares at their par value, and perhaps at less, and so, by gradually investing his savings, will increase his interest in the capital stock.

In all organizations on this plan of partnerships,

the capitalist would probably be careful not to include workmen of an inferior order, or such as would be likely to obstruct or embarrass sound regulations in the administration of work or business. The method would doubtless demand the association of men of sufficient culture to appreciate the necessity of submission to wholesome business rules. It is not probable that the class of men who are most likely to complain of the labour question, and dwell much on its hardships, would find occupation with this kind of association. But to men of industrious, prudent and upright habits, there seems to be no better method of co-operation, and that so well provides for harmony between labour and capital, in the class of larger industries. This, with what may be done in those industries that require no capital beyond that controlled by the workmen themselves, seems to be all that can be done to settle the conflict between labour and capital.

I do not see how this question can be better settled, than by the methods above suggested ; and it is evident these, except so far as the labour and capital of a private firm can accomplish the end, must be largely dependent on the assent of the capitalist. They will not hazard their capital on any plan that does not offer reasonable prospect for remuneration.

If they form a partnership corporation, they will

be cautious in securing workmen of the most reliable character. Now it cannot be disputed there is a pretty large class of workmen who have not the character for self-control that would admit them into such a partnership. Some of these are skilful workmen, but have not the steadiness of habit necessary for such a partnership. It must be kept in mind that all co-operative associations must, to be successful, be made up of men who would be most likely to do well in individual enterprise.

As before observed, skilful, industrious and frugal men will have no difficulty in making thrift that will place them on a comparatively independent basis. But the men who spend their earnings for present gratification, and have none of that regard for future wants which can induce them to lay aside a portion of their earnings, and so prepare for the contingencies of trade or other unavoidable occurrences that contract employment, or arrest ability to work, must suffer more or less when such contingencies overtake them. Very little experience is necessary to admonish men of the changeable circumstances of life, and the necessity for improving what is favourable to-day, in anticipation of at least a possible change to a less favourable condition to-morrow. A provident regard for the future is an essential feature that distinguishes civilization from barbarism. Our civilization has not wholly freed us from an improvident class, and these must be regarded as deficient in mental and moral culture. " As a man soweth, so shall he also reap." There is no escape from this : it is a law of nature and confirmed by revelation. It involves the idea that every man is to provide for himself, and that for this provision he is individually responsible, and cannot evade it without a sacrifice of his manhood. So long as he has the full liberty to apply his labour and his enterprise according to his own judgment, he can have no ground of complaint. If he wastes his earnings on the gratification of present desire, he has no legitimate right to call on his more prudent neighbour, in times of reverse, to make good his imprudence ; and any such call must rest as an appeal to the charity of the prudent.

ABILITY FOR SAVING.

It is sometimes, and I may say often alleged, that working-men do not obtain sufficient wages to have anything left for thrift. Many facts, that any man may observe, go to prove this erroneous as a general principle. It is reported as statistically correct, that there is annually expended in this country, six hundred millions of dollars for intoxicating drinks ; and it is estimated that four hundred millions, beyond any beneficial use of this, is by working-men. It is well known the thrifty class pay a very small proportion of this, probably not one quarter. If this estimate is correct, and I think it fully so, then we have three hundred millions uselessly expended on this item by the improvident class.

I know of no estimate of the number of this class, and do not suppose any great accuracy can be had as to the same. I do not think it exceeds one and a half million of men; but to assume it at double this, or three millions, appears to me quite liberal as to the number. On a cautious basis I therefore take it at three millions, and this gives an average of one hundred dollars for each man per year. This I think too high for common labourers; but it is well known that many skilled labourers indulge in this habit. This estimate embraces only the loss in the actual cost of the liquor drank. In addition to this source of loss, there is much time and health wasted, and money expended by the improvident class, in various useless and more or less demoralizing amusements, and at idle corners and for tobacco. There can therefore be no doubt that more than three hundred millions of dollars per year could easily be saved by this class, and not curtail their necessary expenses one cent.

These sources of saving leave no doubt of the safety of the above estimate. It is amply within the reach of the dependent class. (That the above is a moderate estimate will be manifest, when it is considered the statistics of value are based on the wholesale rate, and that the consumers for the most part pay nearly double this.)

That sum annually saved would provide a capital sufficient to build and equip (1,500) fifteen hundred mills at a cost of ($200,000) two hundred thousand dollars each, or for the purchase of (150,000) one hundred and fifty thousand farms at ($2,000) two thousand dollars each. To bring this question home, I will make the application to the State of New York. This State has about one-ninth, but for round numbers assume that it has one-tenth, of the population of the Union. Then, this rate of saving, practised for ten years, would provide as above, namely, for (1,500) fifteen hundred mills at a cost each of ($200,000) two hundred thousand dollars—or for the purchase of (150,000) one hundred and fifty thousand farms at ($2,000) two thousand dollars each. It is therefore seen the proposed saving would add greatly to the instruments of labour in the hands of labouring-men. It would not only result in this large saving in means, but would also be a saving of the health impaired, and of time wasted and happiness destroyed by the inevitable effects of indulging in intoxicating drinks. And what is more important, it would raise the character of the improvident class, and make them what they should be, the proper guardians and protectors of the happiness, education and respectability of their families —elevate them in their social and political standing with their fellow-men, manifesting in their own persons the real dignity of labour.

This result is in the power of that portion of working-men who most especially complain of the hardships of their lot, and call for the earnest effort of the philanthropist to relieve them from the result of their own improvidence. Industrious perseverance in the saving that may be secured by every able-bodied man, will steadily and surely reduce the ratio of the class of dependent men to that of the class of independent men. The former surrounding themselves as the latter do, with comfortable dwellings, and the means of material and moral improvement; giving them the dignity of manhood and self-control ; furnishing them with improved instruments for their labour and enterprise ; or the investment of their accumulations in interest-paying securities; laying a foundation for the necessities of advancing age, when the ability of labour must necessarily be diminished.

Men, if they would prosper, must be free, and one of the conditions of freedom is, to secure each man in the full enjoyment of his individual personality. In this it is his right to make the best of his situation. If he is industrious, skilful and frugal, barring extraordinary circumstances, he will succeed. If he has not the manliness to do this, he must reap the due reward of his election.

Civilization is the result of culture, and there can be no civilization without the rights of private property ; and property can only be had by industry and frugality. It is substantially all obtained in this way, and those not willing to practice this method, cannot ordinarily expect to obtain it. However well a man may labour, if he spends all his earnings in providing for current wants, he cannot accumulate, and must eventually come to the condition of the dependent class.

It is said some men have a natural turn or gift for thrift, and that others never seem able to get beyond a supply of present wants. No doubt there is a difference in the intellect and moral stamina of men, which it may not be possible for man to equalize or adjust. I do not enter on those cases, but direct my attention to the large proportion who can be improved, as I hope, by mental and moral culture. The differences that appear show the moral of the men, as devel-

oped mostly by education.   In general the case does
not lay in fortune, but in a purpose that makes the
difference we find in society.   The best philanthropy
in this case is, to promote such culture as will establish thoroughly in the mind the principle of self-control, by which a man shall have the power of appro-
priating his energies to useful purposes and guard him
against waste.   When this is effectually secured, there
will be little complaint of the conflict between labour
and capital.

It is certainly no pleasure to set forth the above
remarks, as cause in producing the dependent class ;
but convinced of their truth, I see no alternative.   The
evil of improvidence can only be corrected by fully
unfolding and understanding the cause.

The law of nature, no less than that of revelation,
establishes the rule of right and wrong, and the con-
sequences that inevitably result, as a man makes his
election to follow the one course or the other.   It is
therefore clearly incumbent on every man to deliberate
carefully on the course he will pursue ; as when entered upon he cannot escape the issue.   It is a matter in
which he must take his own responsibility.   There is
no escape from this.

The man who has been well trained in habits of
diligent industry, uprightness, self-control and frugality,

barring exceptional cases, will be thrifty, and rise to competent independence, if not to great wealth. On the other hand, if the man pursues industry merely to satisfy present wants, and with no special regard to the future, he must be content to take his position in the dependent class, and sooner or later realize that his sustenance must come from public or private charity. Every sane man will consider this question, so far as he values his future prosperity. It may be added his present happiness as well ; for no man who has a laudable desire to frugally improve the present, will fail to realize a far greater degree of present enjoyment, than the one who is listless as to the future. It is in this choice the moral tone will be manifested, and the true dignity of manhood be demonstrated. To evade this question on a plea of incompetence, is pusillanimous, and a giving up of all that is manly or characteristic of the essential principles that should call out and adorn individual personality. If any man has not the appreciation of the benefits of civilization so as to induce him to embrace them, and lay the foundation of the prosperity that is within his reach, he will in a greater or less degree follow that of the savage, who will not work to-day for the supply of his wants to-morrow.

It is a common complaint among workmen, that their

wages are too small to allow them to make savings above expenses of living. But this has been done by farm labourers, who in the course of ten years have accumulated by saving from their wages, and the interest thereby secured, from ten hundred to fifteen hundred dollars. This enabled them to purchase a small farm, or to make a large payment down, and thereafter to work as their own masters. The class of men who do this will not stop saving when they enter on their own lands, but will continue to accumulate, and in most cases acquire a handsome independence as a substantial comfort for their advanced years. If this result may be reached by a farm labourer, certainly a skilled labourer may reach a similar independence. All that is needed in either case is the moral nerve or self-control necessary to overcome desire for indulgence in things that are not necessary, and not consistent with ultimate good. It is well for all to consider what has been stated, that this is the way existing capital has mostly been obtained. More or less favourable conditions, and eminence in executive ability, will produce corresponding results. But I have taken the farm labourer or his equivalent as an illustration of what has been accomplished ; and what has been done may still be done, when there is a purpose of making the best of the situation.

Regarding capital, as for the most part it is, the product of accumulated earnings, frugally husbanded, and that the field of similar enterprise is open to all who have the spirit and manliness to embrace it, there can be no just ground for a conflict between it and labour. As an illustration : I employ a man at wages from which he saves more than half his pay. I pay him out of the savings I have accumulated in early life. If I had not in this way provided the capital to pay, he could not obtain the wages from me, nor from any one who had not the capital or means to pay, There is no conflict between me and my workman. I am satisfied with his work, and he is satisfied with his wages, and by his frugality he is accumulating capital.

The conflict that arises between the workman and the capitalist is precisely the same as that which arises in all free commercial transactions between men ; it is in no sense peculiar, and must be settled by the same law of demand and supply that pertains to every department of business. Therefore, though there may be contest, it is in no special sense a conflict. Any effort to evade the law referred to, will inevitably end in failure.

Thrifty and Unthrifty.

There is no question as to the fact that there are two classes in society—The Thrifty and the Unthrifty. It is the province and the duty of Christian civilization to reduce the ratio of the latter to the former. The best progress in this will be made when a practical Christianity has a controlling influence on the minds of men. Vice will inevitably prevail where a sense of moral right and purity does not control. A sound propriety of conduct cannot be expected to prevail in the absence of veneration for the right in affairs, and purity in morals. I know very well there are those, and among them some who have made success in their affairs, that lightly esteem the above sentiment, and claim that principle the best, "that keeps what they have got and gets what they can," leaving others to do as they can with no sympathy from them. Indeed some regard the dependent poor as a necessity for the accommodation of the rich, and treat any desire in them to rise to respectable conditions as an unwarrantable assumption. Such have no fellowship, and ignore the duty and obligation of "doing as they would have others do to them." However men may trifle with these sound principles of morals and of right, they, nevertheless, are the basis of all that is true in our

civilization, and especially in so far as this must be
our reliance, to establish productive industry on a just
basis, and also for the maintenance of civil liberty
and the just rights of men. Disregard for the just
rights of others, for courteous deportment and for
purity of manner, will inevitably lead to anarchy, oppression, and the destruction of the basis on which civilized society rests.

As it has been, so we must expect it will be, these
two classes, the thrifty and the unthrifty, will be more
or less in antagonism with each other. The man that
is unthrifty, who has consumed his earnings as fast as
he has received them, and left no reserve for the wants
of the future, when the future arrives will think it
quite becoming his wants should be supplied out of
the savings of his thrifty neighbour, and complain if
his neighbour does not respond to the necessities of a
fellow-being who comes to him in his time of need.
The unthrifty man takes no note to explain the
wasteful character of his own proceedings, nor regards
the diligence and self-control or self-denial that has
secured to the thrifty man his ability to afford relief.
The unthrifty man attributes his condition to bad luck,
or some inscrutable providence, and by no means refers
it to any remissness or want of providence on his own
part.

We may congratulate ourselves, that of our people, who are for the most part working people, there is so large a proportion of the thrifty class. These hold up our civilization, and so far resist and counteract the tendencies of the other class, as to maintain order in society, and so largely secure the benefits of diligent and economical application in industry and prudence in habit.

So long as that thing called sin (of which some people do not like to speak) has prevalence in the world, there will be strong necessity to originate and maintain the most efficient methods to promote mental and moral culture as a means to mitigate the tendency, if we may not wholly remove the habits of indolence and waste, and so reduce the ratio of the unthrifty to the thrifty to the lowest possible quantity. When this can be made complete we shall have solved the problem of labour and capital in the only way, and to the greatest extent, that is practicable. No American youth should think this beyond his powers. It has been accomplished by vast numbers, as is manifest by the large aggregate wealth that has been produced by the steady diligence and self-control of individual men who had the manliness to make the most of their situation.

All men are not so educated as to appreciate the

above sentiment. The stream will not rise above the fountain. If parents have not the self-control to guide themselves in the right way, how can they be expected to instruct their children ? The man who has not been able to restrain himself, and bring his own powers under the control of reason, can hardly be expected to restrain and guide his children. If the parent is indolent and wasteful, if dishonest in the conduct of his affairs, his children will most probably follow his example. In this we must not forget those parents who have the sense to see their want of education, and make manly efforts to provide it for their children. Such should have all the aid society can give to encourage their laudable endeavour.

In the following section I shall endeavour to present some hints on the benefit of

EDUCATION.

I know there is some authority against me, but I assume the ground that mental and moral culture tends to promote justice, right and purity of manners ; and that the cultivated man is most likely to be industrious and prudent. Exceptions may be quoted showing that intelligence of mind has been connected with great wrongs, and that cultivation gives a manifest power to do a mischief that an uncultured man would be incapable of doing. I am compelled to admit the exception ; but I contend it is only an exception, and does not disturb the general rule ; and hence I look to our public schools and other institutions of learning as the instrumentality for elevating the working class, which in fact includes the most of us as a people. These means are most beneficial when supplemented by sound and discreet family training.

The youth will be ardent and more or less frivolous and frolicsome, and will not be likely to seriously regard the usefulness of his activities. It is in the training of the family these energies are to be mould-ed and their application gradually directed to useful purposes. It is often said youth are heedless and impatient of control, which is true to a large extent. They have not the experience of age, and their ignor-ance leads them to suppose they are wiser than their seniors, or at least quite as wise. Of course these views will be corrected by years, when experience will teach them how small their wisdom was. But it is important they learn as much as practicable before they are called to the responsibility of conducting affairs for themselves. They are not so callous as some suppose, and will learn as they listen from time to time to the instruction, and observe the experience of a discreet parent. A youth will rarely be found who disregards the intelligent counsel of a parent he has learned to respect for his judgment and correct deportment, and is withal impressed by his desire to do him good. The youth that does not respect such a father offers little hope for his future.

The youth not restrained by the fear of God, will hardly understand the full value of justice, or hold that sense of individual responsibility which is necessary to a proper self-reliance. A good character is predicated on doing "justice and judgment," and the exercise of all our powers in industrious production, with a discreet frugality in all our personal appropriations. Self-control should be earnestly and systematically inculcated. To succeed in this, it is indispensable that we exercise the power necessary to subdue those passions which, if unrestrained, bring men under an iron vassalage to vice and prodigality, and as a consequence to poverty. Virtue or vice—this is the real question—"Choose ye which ye will serve."

In all education, the parent should remember the old rule, "It is good for a man to bear the yoke in his youth." If the boy is petted, and fails to obtain a wholesome discipline in his youth, he will probably learn its importance when age will not allow him to profit from its salutary culture. The parent that deals to his children candy and

plums, and stimulates vain desires instead of sub-
jecting them to a healthy discipline, must not expect
from them care and kindness, when age and infirmity
demand this return for parental care, or any comfort
from seeing them in the occupation of high positions
of usefulness among men.   This matter of discipline
is often hard to practice, and demands careful thought
and steady perseverance ; but all experience proves it
is an indispensable requisite to mould the youthful mind,
and bring it to the ultimate enjoyment of a course
of life which at first was regarded with repugnance.

Let no parent who is so far under the influence of
civilization as to feel its power, neglect the above sugges-
tions. They demand the careful consideration of every
parent who expects or desires his son to be educated
in the knowledge of his vocation, and in that firmness
of character that will give him the power to pursue
his calling in such vigorous manner as will secure him
a position among his fellow-men, of at least competence in property, and respectability as a capable
and upright man.   So far as the parent succeeds in
establishing this culture, he will bring this contest
between labour and capital to an end by a durable
peace.   No material gains can be of so great value, or
do his son so much good, as a well-formed character,
with ability for useful occupation.

INEQUALITY IN WEALTH.

Property, during the historic period, has mostly been in the hands of a comparatively small number of men. Its diffusion in society has increased as civilization in general culture has advanced. It is therefore evident that culture, by the education of every working-man, is eminently important for progress in the civilization necessary to promote the general well-being of society. Culture renders man dissatisfied with what is barely sufficient for necessary subsistence, and he is led to seek enlargement in his wants. The savage is content with a hut, culture demands a house with apartments. As new wants are presented to his tastes or called to increase his comforts, the cultivated man seeks or devises some new or more efficient method of industry as the means of providing them. His ingenuity is stimulated to ascertain the method, and his perseverance opens by degrees the path to his object. In his progress, what was at first regarded as a luxury, becomes a common necessity. This progress developes taste and enterprise, brings out the arts that elevate the mind and improves civilization. In its course it leads to additional sources of industry, calling in the power of mechanical agents to aid the labour of men in the productions that minister to their wants. These additional sources of industry and power, enlarge the field of employment to both labour and capital.

As before observed, it does not always happen that labour and capital are in the same hands. One party has capital and the other labour and skill, and these must be harmonized on some principle that will regulate their respective positions. In the case where the capitalist is not a professional manufacturer, and the workman is not able to command the means necessary to conduct the operations on his own account ; the question with the capitalist will be—can I obtain a better interest for my funds by erecting mills and conducting the manufacture of a certain fabric, than by other means of investment? The prospect must be such as will secure an affirmative answer, or he will depend on other ways of using his funds. He may be mistaken in his conclusion ; but this answer is necessary before he makes the decision to erect the necessary works. As a matter of business, he is justified in estimating the cost of the labour he will require, on the current rate of the market for wages. It is no part of his concern to investigate the rate of wages that will support the workman ; that is altogether a matter for the workman himself. The latter, in his right, will consider his interest, in view of all the circumstances of the case, in the light of the labour market ; on the same principle the former looks to the market rate of interest for his funds. It is on both sides a purely commercial transaction. There are no equities in this, except so far as may regard the proper and just discharge of the obligation of contract between the parties; they negotiated on the basis of commercial equality; and are equally bound to fidelity in the execution of their contracts, same as in any business. The charity view must be thrown out altogether as having no part in the matter. If there be any circumstance that calls for charity or benevolence, it must be treated as a gratuity, and so far removed from the domain of business.

There must of necessity be "inequality in wealth." The discreet man, who by prudently husbanding his resources has come to mature years surrounded by a well-arranged and productive property, which affords him a comfortable independence, according to his education and taste, we may suppose has raised a family, of perhaps a half a dozen children. He is able to provide for this family according to the habits in which they have been educated. Now the time will come when this estate must be divided. As a compact whole, it was ample to provide under one roof for this family ; but in the division, this well-ordered unit of estate, will be less valuable than before the division. The children must now be content to take each his fragment, which will probably be quite inadequate to support them separately in the style and manner they had been accustomed to under the paternal roof. If now they have been well trained to some useful vocation, they will supplement, each his own fragment, by industry and prudence, and with the aid of their patrimony, judiciously add to its volume, and very probably reach a higher . degree of wealth than the parent. But if, as is not unfrequent, they feel so well provided for as to demoralize their industry, and give a slack view to exertions, failing of the effort required to make the necessary thrift, they will very probably exhaust their patrimony and become poor indeed. If the patrimony be so large as to be sufficient, with no more effort than required for its preservation, it is still important to exercise prudence, and secure at least some degree of thrift. This is important in view of losses that may occur from investments, even if no increased expenses are anticipated, as it will provide means for making good any loss that may occur, and so keep good the income. Here is an obvious source of inequality.

But the main source of inequality in wealth is

found in the two classes of men—the thrifty and the unthrifty. One of these will manage affairs by saving, and so accumulate wealth—the other elects to consume all his earnings, and has little or nothing for accumulation. The inevitable result is, the thrifty man has wealth, and the unthrifty man passes through life in daily struggle for little or nothing above a bare subsistence. This is the result of individual character. One man improves his powers and another does not, and inequality is the inevitable result. No device of man, or perfection in civilization has thus far been sufficient to prevent this, and it is incumbent on all men to so perfect education as will remove this evil, so far as it may be practicable to do so.

This Conflict not Peculiar.

Although capital and labour must, to a large extent, work together in the production of fabrics, there is no doubt a conflict of interest, same as in any business transaction; but in no way peculiar to this. The capitalist desires to obtain the largest interest he can for his funds, and the workman seeks to obtain the highest wages the market will command for his labour. There can be no objection to this in either case, nor is it different from the struggle that pertains to all business under commercial freedom.

Combinations or Monopolies.

The principle of combination to maintain a certain rate of wages, is the same as that to maintain a certain price for goods. In either case, if the respective parties are agreed, they may combine their interests, and refuse any transaction that does not accord with their purpose. So far it is merely a voluntary affair, depending on the mutual confidence of the parties.

The courts will not take cognizance of such combinations, with a view to inflict damage on any of the parties connected, if they choose to break from the combination, and conduct their affairs independently. The rule of law that governs in such cases is, that the combination is inconsistent with public policy. Any action, therefore, of the combination that aims to punish those outside, or even one within, if he choose to conduct his affairs independently, will be held unlawful, and punished as any other wrong-doing. This principle of law is essential to civilization and the maintenance of the commercial freedom that is indispensable to the just rights, as well as the paramount interests of society. It is quite as important for securing the right of the workmen, as for that of the capitalist. This has no relation to contracts for service in labour or other exchange, but to those efforts in combination which aim to overthrow the laws of commercial freedom, either by monopoly or any forestalling of the market.

Combinations have often been formed to control the rate of wages and the price of goods. At the present day, the means of communication are so enlarged, that combinations require too wide a scope to be successfully conducted for any considerable length of time. The varied circumstances of individuals and localities will tend to break in ; and as no legal power exists to control or enforce them, they soon fall, and all parties are brought into submission to the laws that regulate demand and supply. To this result, if there is no speciality in the case, all such efforts must come, and it is not only the most just, but the best rule that has been found. If the supply of capital is large in proportion to demand, the rate of interest will be low, and the same rule holds in relation to the rate of wages. The party that desires to hire funds or labour, will pay no more than may be necessary to command either funds or labour. In either case, business is done on this basis.

To a widow who has a thousand dollars to invest, it may be very desirable, and perhaps important for her to obtain ten per cent per year; but if the market will only give five per cent, she must be content with five. Precisely the same to a workman.

It may be important for him to obtain two dollars for a day's labour, but if the supply of labour is so abundant he can find no offer over a dollar, he must take the dollar, on the same principle the widow accepts five per cent for her funds. In either case if more is paid in interest or wages, it must be as a charity; and this removes the question from the category of business, a method that has no basis in the commercial affairs of men. The charity view, moreover, is derogatory to the workman, degrading the dignity of labour.

An intelligent and enterprising workman will see that capital is only the accumulated savings gathered from previous labour and frugality; and that his savings will be his own capital, as will be manifest as he gathers the proceeds of his own enterprise and prudence, and which will work for him either as instruments in his business or as interest on invested capital gathered from his savings.

This Conflict Should be Adjusted.

If it were not frequently said—the conflict between labour and capital must be settled, we should conclude the matter must be adjusted on the same basis as all other commercial transactions. What, then, can be meant by settling the conflict between labour and capital? Is there any potentate who by decree can settle this question? It would seem that some people think it a prerogative of government to do this, and some attempts have been made, so far as giving law to the hours that constitute a day's work. Applied to minors, this may be a proper exercise of authority to protect the young from improper exactions of employers or guardians ; but as applied to men, who hold the power of citizenship, and the full right of contract, is no more just or proper than for government to fix the price of a barrel of flour or a pound of meat. In the latter case it assumes that an adult man is not a free agent, and has no real personality, and needs the paternal care of the government to minister to his daily necessities.

Not far in the past, it was regarded necessary that the weight of a shilling loaf of bread should be determined by municipal authority. This was the practice not many years since in the city of New York, and in other cities. What was termed the " assize of bread," was a measure to protect the consumers from imposition by the bakers. It was adjusted from time to time as the price of flour changed in the market. I very well recollect hearing this subject discussed by citizens of New York, about thirty-five years ago, who said they found the assize to be useless—that the competition among the bakers was the best regulation. And so, gradually the people bought their bread from the baker who gave the best in weight and quality, and the assize by municipal authority was abandoned: it fell by its own dead weight, an exploded relic of the past.

In former days it was regarded necessary for the city to build markets, for the sale of provisions, and to protect the people ; certain persons were licensed to furnish and sell the same by authority. No one was allowed to sell who had not a license, and at the regular market of the city. This was then regarded necessary to protect the citizens from imposition in the supply of their daily wants of meat, poultry, vegetables, fish, fruits, &c. The city of New York has largely grown since those days, and with its growth markets have been established and conducted by individual enterprise at the stores of the owners, without license, in various parts of the city, and now constitute the principal sources of supply for the daily wants of the citizens. Thus as time and intelligence advanced, municipal regulations have given place to free trade. The city and its vicinity now contains about one and a half million of people, whose daily wants are supplied by the untrammelled law of supply and demand. All this is done quietly ; no one

of this vast population takes thought where his supplies may come from ; he goes to the store or market
not doubting he will find gathered all things in their
season. And how is the daily supply for this population gathered ? There is no government organization.
No authority is constituted to gather supplies. If it
were an army of troops, what a busy going to and fro
of commissaries and assistants ; what hurry and worry
of transport and distribution would pervade the surrounding country ; and who can imagine the amount
of corruption that would swell the expenses through
this instrumentality? But this great population is
provided for without commotion or excitement, and
finds its daily wants supplied without the least effort
as to the source or order by which they are brought to
hand ; and all under the silent operations of the law
of demand and supply.

Contemplate the great population of New York
and vicinity, in view of the daily supplies that are
needed, and all supplied in such a quiet way that no
one inquires beyond the market for the article he
wants, nor feels any regulating authority of government to aid or embarrass him. The old laws of assize
of bread, and market license, have ceased, and the city
presents a beautiful specimen of the order, efficiency
and economy of the laws of free trade, operating on a

large scale. They have quietly superseded the method of municipal regulation, which has been found inferior, and has given place to natural law.

Now, if government authority has failed to prove useful in regulating the value of bread, and the sale of provisions in a large city, the absolute necessities for every day for all, what possible chance is there that it can regulate the intricate relations of labour and capital with any more beneficence? There can be none at all. Any proposition to adjust these relations by other power than the law of demand and supply will fail. Other projects may originate in benevolent views towards labour, but they will prove mistaken views, that neither do credit to the workmen nor justice to the dignity of labour. They repudiate the principle of self-government, and go to establish what is termed paternal government, or one that holds man incapable of conducting his own affairs. Government is certainly necessary, in order that every man be protected in his own personal rights, and secure to each his rights of labour and contract. After this the man should be left free to conduct his affairs according to his own judgment, under equal laws.

Labour cannot be employed, unless there is an object to serve. It is wanted when there is work to be done, and will be employed if the market rate warrant the production for which it is desired. If this is too high to justify its application to the specific object, then this class of production cannot be prosecuted, and the labour must seek another channel for employment. Is it possible under such circumstances for the government to step in and direct the course of industries. No sensible man will claim this. If therefore labour is in excess of the demand, the tendency will be the same as in all over supply of goods or services, and subject to the same competition. There is no possible escape from this, without destroying the basis of commercial freedom.

No labour is bestowed nor funds appropriated to any production, except on the basis of deriving a profit. Neither will be supplied, unless the prospect of remuneration is equal to that which may be obtained in other branches of industry. To say to a workman, you must work for a fixed rate, or to a capitalist you must be content with a fixed profit, irrespective of the market, is absurd and injurious to all parties, though governments have more or less attempted such regulations. But this paternity principle is on the wane, and will be wholly abandoned as intelligence prevails. If this is correct, how shall the labour and capital problem be solved ? These parties will not go into production on any other terms than the market rate, unless some arbitrary power should interpose to compel them. Any such power would destroy self-government or civil liberty, and reduce man to dependence on a despot. But we are by no means left to this alternative. The law of demand and supply is ample for the adjustment of this question. Let these alone, and with the greatest harmony they will work out the best possible result in the combined operations of labour and capital. This is commercial freedom, the only law that can secure dignity and just remuneration to labour, and the proper return for capital. Both are to be compensated on the basis of this one law, and no act of man can produce a more beneficent result, and all efforts to evade it can only end in failure or despotism.

Some men discuss this question as though we should have a bashaw to determine and settle the intricacies of our industries. This is claimed in the interest of labour, as though it was some feeble thing that had not the power to take care of itself. What is the great fact of American history in regard to labour ? It is that it has produced nearly all the capitalists of the country,—has subdued a wilderness, and in place erected dwellings, offices, warehouses and mills ; it has built cities, canals and railways ; it has drained and fenced the lands, so that our eyes behold a cultivated country. In addition, it has built school-houses, academies, colleges, and sustained the education that has given us our civilization; it has erected church edifices and sustained the preaching of the gospel of Christ, which is the constitution of civil liberty. After all this shall labour go begging for charity? Heaven forbid!

But to this it is replied, will you not allow the exercise of charity to the unfortunate? Certainly, not only to the unfortunate, but also to the improvident; it is proper for the government and for individuals to make provision for the aged, the infirm, and all that from mental or physical imbecility are unable to provide for their own subsistence. But this takes the question out of the business circle, and we must be careful not to confound manly labour with pauperism.

To an American citizen it will readily occur that this question is intimately connected with civil liberty. Free government is supposed to be established for the purpose of securing to every man, by equal laws, the rights of labour and enterprise; with no class privileges. It is founded on the belief that every man will judge most wisely of the kind or method of labour best suited to his circumstances. This is the highest hope of the working-man. It puts him in the position to make the best of his situation. It is for him to de-

11

cide whether or not he will occupy its advantages. Here is a field open to the cultivation and improvement of his best powers. Though he begin in a small way, with patient perseverance and prudent conduct of his affairs, he will take thrift from the start, and gradually improve his condition, until he reach a reasonable competence if not large wealth. If, however, the government by some Utopian method takes from his savings, and bestows it on some indolent brother workman, he will so far lose the benefit of his own industry. It is to be observed the government can give nothing to one that it does not take from another, and hence the gross injustice of any such act of special favour. The same result will follow any attempt of authority, to stipulate the terms of labour. Certainly it requires very little reflection to see the impossibility of any just regulation of the intricate affairs of labour and capital, as associated in production by authority of government. The effort to compass this by regulating the hours of labour for adult men, is a gross intermeddling that can only work evil, and is no part of the function of government.

The protection of civil liberty is of the most important benefit to all labour and enterprise, and should be especially cherished by the working-man, who should be jealous of any infringement of his natural

right or the establishment of any class privileges in
society. This question of civil liberty deserves to be
carefully considered by every working-man. It involves the very important principle of individuality or
free government by which each citizen is sustained in
the right of employing his energies in such a way as
he regards most likely to promote his welfare. Now,
what other power can so well understand this as himself? Who else shall so fully comprehend the numerous circumstances, of business by which he may be
surrounded ? Is it possible for government to do this ?
It is a well-settled principle, that affairs conducted by
government are more expensive than those conducted by an individual. And from this it is well claimed
by the friends of civil liberty, that the government
should be restricted in its operations to those things
that cannot be conducted by individuals. Even a
business corporation is more exposed to errors in
judgment and corruption in management, than those
managed by an individual, or a firm of two or three
persons.

Government is wanted to maintain justice among
men, and protect each from any wrong on the part of
others ; and this should be irrespective of parties ; establishing protection to all, and granting special favours
to none. Civil liberty rests on the doctrine " that all

men are by nature free, and possess the inalienable right of life, liberty and the pursuit of happiness." This principle is all-important to the working-man, and in fact to all others as well. It sustains, in full action, the power of individual labour and enterprise, giving to man the right to make the most of his situation. Under this rule our country has prospered. Industry has been rewarded, and men with nothing but their skill and labour to begin with, have acquired large wealth, and great numbers have obtained competent estates. But it must not be forgotten these results have been secured by industry and frugality—beginning with small thrift and followed up under the influence of a wise self-control. This class have no conflict with capital. They feel the strength of individual power. The conflict is confined mostly to the class who labour for present subsistence, and are not disposed to restrain the gratification of to-day in order to secure a future good. These are very likely to complain of their lot, and look enviously to those of their fellow-workmen who by self-denial have been thrifty, and by this very means have put tools and machinery into the hands of their less provident fellows, thereby saving the latter from the necessity of depending on the chase to procure the means of a scanty and precarious subsistence.

Industry and frugality are the basis of thrift; they are of eminent benefit, not only to the individual that practices them, but to society in general. It is not merely in the accumulation of property, but is also of great value in promoting the mental and moral advancement of men. The man who has a purpose to improve his condition, by every laudable means in his power, has put on a powerful shield for his protection against the evils and degradation of ignorance and vice.

Every American working-man should deeply consider the benefit he enjoys in the possession of civil liberty, in that it secures to him the right to exercise his industry in the way he regards most beneficial to himself. If in this he fails to make the best use of his powers, he should not complain of those who do. It he possess ordinary powers, or such as place him above the plane of charity, he must consider the world owes him nothing but justice and fair dealing. It is his province to provide for himself by the laudable and vigilant exercise of his own powers. The motto, "that the world owes him a living," is without foundation, and strikes at the basis of individuality.

It is sometimes said property is very unequally distributed. This is largely, if not essentially, an error, when applied to young men, who rarely have much property in the outset of life. If applied to those of advanced age, it merely expresses the fact— that all men do not equally avail of the facilities for thrift, that have arisen from the industry and prudence of those who have been successful.   One man carefully husbands his resources, while another spends more than is needful in the indulgence of present desire.

As to young men it may be said there are those who obtain property from the savings of their parents, and thus have a property to commence their business life.   While this is true to some extent, it is doubtful if such inheritance gives them any advantage over the young man who, having no expectations of this kind, manfully prepares for his business life, and depending on his personal energy and skill, pursues his vocation with greater vigour.   It is often found that the expectation of inheritance impairs close attention to business, and often leaves the race to him who had only his better cultivated individual power.   It is difficult for a young man who has never known much of want to realize the necessity of the energy and prudence required to conduct labour or business with thrift. It therefore appears the best thing a parent can do for his son, is to carefully instruct him in a business education, so as to well fit him for the calling he is intended to follow.   There is no more pleasant thing for a parent than to see his son go forward in his occupation and gradually rise in character as a capable, intelligent and upright citizen. This he may reasonably hope for if his education in business and purity of manners has been correct and well impressed, whether he have property to begin with or not.

There have been instances of men rising in disregard of their surroundings to a rank of prominence in business life. But these are exceptional cases ; the great mass of men will move on in the path they have chosen according to their education ; and the probability of correcting cardinal errors of youth in time to profit, is very small, and hence the importance of correct early training. This training must depend essentially on the parent. The young man goes into his business life according to his training. As a matter of course this will depend on the capacity of the parent for the work. It will require a good degree of self-control and perseverance. In the nature of the boy there will be much to correct in order to mould him into conformity with the exigencies of a business life. The first important point to be considered is, the son does not know as much as the father, and therefore the father should put himself in the position of an instructor, and should consider, that no one knows, in a practical degree, by intuition, and if the son does not know, it is because he has not seen or heard and is in need of information. A wise parent will always avail of any circumstances, even in the common routine of every-day affairs, to bring knowledge to the opening mind of his son, so as to fortify him against error, and illustrate truth to his mind.

Ordinary elementary education is not here under consideration ; but the education of business life, the formation of the mind to the exigencies of business affairs.   No great experience is required to know there are many contingencies that hang around and render uncertain the result of enterprise ; all demanding prudence to guard against disappointment.   Often a very promising enterprise ends in severe loss.   All such results afford experience, and the young man should be guarded as much as possible against such losses by the warning of a father's experience.   The father has more or less of experience from his own transactions, and his observation on those of other men.   To be useful to his son he should communicate to him his own knowledge in all matters that come under his observation.   Boys that have had proper training will ordinarily be very attentive to the advice and instruction of a parent who has instilled confidence in his efforts to impart useful instruction.   I know it is said

boys are vain and self-willed, thinking they are wiser
than their seniors ; but I have seldom known a boy
that did not listen with respect to the instruction of
an intelligent and discreet parent. The boy has passions and appetites that often urge him in opposition
to wholesome advice, and when these tendencies are
opposed by severe terms, the effect is often unfavour-
able ; but if they are met with a wise moderation, and
a manner that indicates not only the wisdom of
experience but a serious paternal interest in the boy's
prosperity, he will be most likely to yield to wise
counsel before he is aware of it.

To forewarn a son against errors in business pur-
suits, and impress on his mind the necessity of caution and propriety of manners, and in all matters of
doubt to advise him to consult with men of experience,
in whose integrity he may confide, is an important
parental duty. It is favourable that a large portion of
the affairs of business life are easily learned ; they are
only complex as a man advances to those operations of
high skill, trust and confidence, that more open the
young man to the influence of deception and errors of
judgment. Here he may need the counsel of a dis-
interested friend, and no one can be found so reliable as a parent. He is naturally concerned, that
his son should not only succeed in his business pur-

suits, but that he establish the character of an intelligent and upright citizen. Among the things a parent should call to the attention of his son are— steady industry, and a care to avoid any expense that will not allow thrift. Thrift or progress elevates the dignity and sustains a man in labour, and renders his work pleasant and interesting, which would otherwise be irksome.

I have known men who by their skill and industry had acquired large property, but failed to so educate their sons as to enable them to preserve and improve it. This is far less favourable than a small property, with a sound business education. Such errors tend to scatter the accumulations of a successful business life, and show the folly of neglecting the business and moral education of children.

After a parent has done all that he may be able to do in the instruction of his son in the business affairs of life, he should not forget the indispensable culture that shall teach him "to fear God and keep his Commandments." This is the great duty of man, and is withal the basis of all prosperity and happiness.

CONCLUSION.

I take exception to the scientific and philanthropic writers on industrial economy, who assume that the labouring men are in an impotent and dependent condition. There is doubtless more ground for such opinion in countries where population has passed to the line of diminishing supplies, and where by law or usage property has special favours. But I am discussing the question from the American stand-point, and especially for the free States of the North American union. I suppose the Dominion of Canada is in much the same condition. At present it can hardly be said the late slave States are properly in a fair condition as to labour; but when those States shall come to manifest a just sense of the rights of men, the dignity of labour will prevail, and they will have an untrammelled industry, and advance to the enjoyment of civil liberty.

In our own country, we have not reached the line of diminishing supplies, and if we are wise, we shall never reach it.

I do not specially criticise the writers of other countries, where circumstances are different from our own. But I do not think there is any excuse for American writers to hold up our working-men as an oppressed and degraded class calling for sympathy. Those writers do admit there may be moral improvement, but this idea they mostly hold as a remote, if not an improbable hope. They admit that here and there one rises from the ranks of working-men to positions of prominence.

I know very well there is a large class of working-men who are in great measure dependent on their employers, and never rise to a comfortable well-being or to a reputable standing in society. No doubt some of these are the subjects of untoward circumstances, and should be treated with a kindly regard ; but for the most part we may trace their condition to their ignorance and improvidence. Even this class must be treated with kindness. On the other hand, there is, not " here and there one," but a large proportion of our working-men, who began life on wages and have reached a respectable competence, and some large wealth ; certainly these cannot be classed as a dependent body, calling for sympathy.

It has been held that a man working for hire cannot rise by any cultivation of his powers from a life of dependence. I have known many exceptions to this statement. Many of the inventions and improvements in the useful arts have been wrought out, more or less, by men working for hire ; who pondered their thoughts in the shops and studied them in their evenings and other intervals of work. I have known men who worked for wages—were excellent workmen, who by occupying their leisure in useful reading and the society of intelligent men, were well informed on general subjects, and able to maintain discussion with intelligent men.

I utterly disapprove and repudiate the Utopian methods of elevating the working-men, by what I regard as misguided sympathy. The working-men do elevate themselves ; and the class among them that call for sympathy may also elevate themselves. Is it not then far better to point out to the working-man the way he can raise himself than to unnerve him by holding up his condition as one of impotent dependence. In this free country he has the power, and if he consider his own good, he will use it, rather than trust his well-being to sentimental impracticabilities.

THE QUESTION OF MARRIAGE.

Writers on industrial economy attribute much of the hardships of the labouring class to early marriages. No doubt there is some foundation for this ; but it is a subject I do not propose to discuss. There are so many circumstances influencing the question of marriage, which each one must consider for himself, that

I do not see in what way I may give advice. This much, however, may be said : in marriage there is necessity of responsibility for the sustenance of wife and children, and the education of the latter. Any provident man will consider if his resources will be sufficient to meet the responsibility involved in these expenses. His judgment in this respect will very probably decide, whether he shall be a thrifty or an unthrifty man.

Some hold this question of early marriage under the aspect of religion. It is not unusual to hear the sentiment, " the Lord will provide." I honor the doctrine of trust in the providence of God ; but I hold it in subordination to the teachings of the Christian Scriptures. Here I find the precept, " Thou shall not tempt the Lord thy God." The husbandman must trust in God for the rain and sunshine that are necessary to make his fruit; but if he fail to cultivate his ground in seed time, " he shall beg in harvest." " He that will not work, neither shall he eat."

From the teaching of the Christian Scriptures it is evident to my mind, that God has given men power of labour and prudence, and that he will hold them to their responsibility for their proper exercise in industry and frugality ; and in their exercise men may expect his favour, and realize his promise, that

" he that gathereth by labour shall increase." It has often appeared to me this sentiment—" the Lord will provide "—is advanced as an apology for doing something that in all rational experience it was not expedient to do, or at least not discreet under the existing condition. Those that yield to such indiscretion may expect disappointment, if they be not thrown into the dependent class. In this I must not be understood as hostile to marriage life ; for I regard it as eminently conducive to human happiness, and also as a fundamental principle in civilization. It is the establishment of mutual confidence, fellowship and interest, most congenial to the happiness of men. It is the cardinal stimulus to effort for advancing the industry and economy that promote the material, mental and moral well-being of society ; and is naturally looked to, as a proper condition in the life of men. But in this, as in every enterprise of men, prudence demands that a man consider, if he have the means to meet its proper responsibilities. If he has not the means, he will probably fail to secure success. All I advise therefore is, that its consummation be deferred until a reasonable prospect is secured for the means of providing for its necessary responsibilities, always leaving something for thrift. I say leaving something for thrift ; for the man who can see no pro-

gress towards improving his affairs, will lose courage
and make life a drudgery.

Desire is importunate, and urges its claims with
persistent energy; presenting in strong terms the necessity and propriety of its claims ; while on the other
hand, the future good that trembles in the balance is
modest, and scarcely dares to confront the energy of
its opponent : depending on the influence of its wisdom and prudence, it will only be heeded by the wise
and discreet that wait on her counsel.   It is an affair
that commends itself to the careful consideration of
every man who has any realizing appreciation of the
individual responsibilities that he must assume in
providing for himself and family, and will most probably shape the course of his life.

That there are many who have difficulty in providing sustenance, and come to depend on public and
private charity, there can be no doubt.   But to charge
their condition to the hard terms imposed on them by
capitalists, is a great error.   The capitalist has done
the same by them as he has done by those who have
risen to the condition of competent independence.
The capitalist has furnished these dependent men
with the instruments of labour, without which they
could have had no civilized work to do ; and must have
been driven to hunting and fishing for the means of

subsistence. The charge against the capitalist is one that strikes at the foundation of our civilization. But, it may be inquired, is there no remedy? Must our civilization be maintained at so great sacrifice as we see in the comparatively large number of dependent men? Is this a necessary result? To answer these questions, we have only to look over our society and see how large the proportion of men who began life with little or no resources but their skill and labour, and have reached competent conditions. How did they reach this condition? It was not by chance, but by industriously and wisely using the instruments put into their hands from the savings accumulated by their predecessors—now called capitalists. If no such instrument had been provided, they must have depended on the scanty resources of nature for the means of subsistence. With the same instruments the prudent man proceeded, until by industry and frugality he provided for his own instruments, and steadily and surely rose to the position of competent independence, if not to that of a large capitalist. The dependent class had the same opportunity—had the benefit of the same instruments, but had not the manly purpose to improve their advantages. They thought the world owed them a living—a great error of men, who forget the world owes them nothing; and that every man, who is not a pauper, is dependent on his own industry and vigilance for the subsistence he needs or desires.

It is a mistake to suppose that in a free country, where labour is untrammelled by unjust laws or usages, there is any hardship in labour as to the two classes under consideration. The two classes are formed by their own unrestricted choice, and all that the government or the philanthropist can do in the premises, is to provide the means of education, so that all may improve on their own natural powers, and be rendered able to make a wise use of the instruments that have been provided, and which make their labour more effective for their own and the public good. An indolent or improvident man will surely come to want.

If we discard civilization, we must fall into barbarism. This latter result will inevitably come if the right of holding and enjoying the savings of frugal industry be denied.

The class of dependent men do not wholly come from those who are entering the responsibilities of life, with only their skill and labour to provide for their well-being. It embraces many who had, in addition to their own industry, more or less of means received from parents and other friends to aid them, but failed to improve their advantages, and fell into poverty. It is not necessary here to discuss the particulars of their failure, as it arose from the same cause that threw the other members into this class ; namely, the want of industry and prudence to improve their advantages.

As I have stated, I do not recommend that the class of dependent men be excluded from sympathy, however they may have arrived at this condition. They should have provision from public and private charity, sufficient for their sustenance ; but this should be provided wisely, so as not to make it a bounty on indolence and improvidence. The " poor laws of England," the most elaborate and extensive of bounty or provision for the poor, are held by intelligent writers who have carefully studied them, as having been an agency that has greatly increased the number of dependent poor.

Civilization cannot properly progress, if it do not call out and stimulate individual character,—call out the energy and moral nerve that gives vigour to all the powers of men, eschews dependence on others, and maintains a manly exercise of personal faculties. So far as we weaken these sentiments, we add to the class of dependent men, and impair the results of industry. There is no other doctrine for a free country.

The writers who complain of our organization of

industry, and insist on some new adjustment that
shall give labour a larger share in production, do not
seem to show any practical method by which their
views may be realized. The law of supply and demand they reject as not equitable, and appear to
content themselves with some impracticable notions
to heal the difficulties they imagine to exist in the
relations of labour and capital. They must certainly
forget that the law of demand and supply is the outgrowth of civilization, founded on the right and propriety of individual judgment, as to whether any
exchange of services or goods is desirable, and conducive to the personal interest of the parties. The
savage will exercise force to compel his fellow to
part with his goods, if he happen to have such as
he wants. He has respect to no other law, and the
weak must yield to the strong. The great beauty of
civilization is, to establish Institutional law, by which
the weak are protected in their rights, and to secure
every one in the personal right of making contract
according as he regards his own interest. To abandon
this principle, would be to throw out of sight the
great fact of civilization, namely, the right of each
man to the full enjoyment of his own industry and
savings, or the right of private property, which cannot
be abandoned without adopting the only alternative,

which is barbarism. If we adopt this alternative, then, the instruments of civilized industry would soon be consumed, and men must come to depend on the chase, and natural fruits for means to sustain a scanty and precarious subsistence, and this for only a comparatively meagre population. It cannot be successfully controverted, that the right of private property is the only stimulus that can sustain efficient industry. If I am right, then, the efforts to show there is some peculiar hardship in labour,—that it has an unequal contest with capital, can have no other effect than to demoralize the labourer, and make him look on his condition as one of peculiar privation, and thus impair his moral power, and with it his prospect of improving his condition. No such doctrine can prevail in a free country, with men who have the purpose to be men.

Who are the Working Class.

In this country, probably nineteen out of every twenty come to adult age with little or no means, except the skill and labour of their vocation. They depend on their manual and mental industry to provide for their sustenance and happiness. It was for the most part the same with their fathers before them. This commencement of individual responsibility calls for the most careful consideration of the plan of life for a young man. He is now to decide whether he will put forth his energies in a manly way, and improve the advantages of the civilization by which he is surrounded, and rise steadily to the condition of an independent man, or whether he will be content to forego those advantages, and heedlessly slide into the class of dependent men. The choice should now be made, as at any future time the decision is most likely to be embarrassed not only by loss of time, but by habits that will offer serious obstacles to success.

If the young man sets out with a look of apprehension that he may not be able to overcome the difficulties he apprehends, and lacks the nerve that is indispensable to success—or if he commences on a plan of life that consumes his earnings as fast as earned, he will in all probability reach his position in the class of dependent men. If he have the weakness to yield to present desire, and not the nerve to control this when in the full strength of his powers, there is no probability he will do so when age has impaired those powers. On the other hand, if he resolutely eschews all indolence and dissipation, expends no means that are not necessary for his reasonable wants, enters no responsibilities until he has the means to meet them without imparing reasonable thrift, he will in all rational probability raise his condition to at least a competent independence. I say from my own experience and observation, to all American young men, this is the choice before you, and your success depends on yourselves.

To some, the course recommended will appear a slow process. Its movement will certainly be slow in the beginning. Let not this discourage the young man. The early tardiness of result will be alleviated as the benefits are unfolded. A cheering and encouraging aspect will accompany the net proceeds of the first year, and though this may not be large, it will be a precursor of what a few years of patient perseverance will do. This is equally important in professional as in manual labour. The great fact must not be lost sight of, namely, this is the way in which, for the most part, capitalists have been made. It is no chimera ; but the fact of our history as a country. It has developed the blessings of free and untrammelled labour, open alike to all, with no special favours to any.

Why then, in this free country, should we hear complaints of capitalists, who have been the strength of our civilization ? By the savings of their industry they have provided the instrumentalities that give efficiency to labour, and more abundantly provide the

elements of well-being to individuals and to society.
Is it not far better to direct our attention to those
educationa limprovements by which we may hope to
raise the dependent to an independent class, and so
enlarge the industrial results by the double process of
increasing production, and at same time diminishing
the necessity for charity in sustaining the dependent
class ?

In speaking of capitalists, I do not confine myself
simply to the larger class, but include also those who
are able to provide instruments for their own labour,
as well as those who are able to provide instruments
for the labour of others. It should not be lost sight
of, that these instruments only exist to any important
extent in a civilized country ; and are accumulated by
persistent labour and prudence. They are the power
that makes labour eminently effective, giving the
highest results in the production of fabrics indispensable for a civilized community. They are not
held, and never can be, as owners, in the hands of the
dependent class. They must be worked for; they are
only accumulated by the thrifty class of working-men,
who have the sagacity to see their value and the
manly nerve to so prosecute their labour as to command
the instruments for their own benefit.

I must not be understood as offering any apology

for whatever may be wrong or oppressive on the part of capitalists, whether they obtain capital by their own or the labour of others. As a class, I do not think they are more inclined to disregard the principles of right than other men. In our free country the laws will essentially protect the labouring man, and any oppression will arouse the indignation of the public in favour of justice. I have been intimate with the circumstances of great numbers of working-men, and have rarely known an instance of a good workman suffering injustice in any large industry. It is a general fact, the competent and faithful workman is cherished as a valuable appendage to any industrial enterprise.

Labour a Necessity.

Labour is a commodity the civilized world cannot dispense with. It is a resource, or a capital in the hands of the labourer, which is a power to elevate him in his moral and material well-being. He has the power to make it useful, same as any other capital, and has only to make a wise improvement of its resources, according to the market demand, and prudently husband its earnings. It enjoys the benefit of the large instrumentalities that civilization has put into its hands. In this free country it has the un-

trammelled right to exercise its full powers, and secure
to itself the full blessings of its application.

The man who commences life with only skill and
labour as his stock in trade, should look up to the
capitalist who furnished the instruments of his work,
and anticipate the day when he will furnish his own
instruments, and thus secure the wages of his labour
and the profits of his instruments. This is far more
noble and inspiring than to listen to the strains of
sentimentalists who take credit to themselves in draw-
ing for the working-man a doleful, if not a hopeless
future, presenting capitalists as the enemies of the labouring man. Be assured this is not true. Consider,
for a moment, what could the labourer do without the
instruments provided for his work ? And where could
the instruments be had if there were no capitalists ?

If there were no instruments, then production
would be impracticable, or require far greater labour
in the few things that could be produced, and society,
including working-men, would have so much less of
the means of subsistence. No, it is not the capitalist that injures labour ; he enlarges the field of its
operations, and increases its productiveness, as can
be testified by great numbers who have by these
means raised themselves to the position of competent
independence. Let any labouring man look candidly

and intelligently into this subject, and notice what his condition would be, if there were none of the instruments of civilization that he could avail of. As a mat· ter of course he must descend into the condition of savage life, as that is the only alternative left for him to take. That would be worse than the dependent condition, as surrounded by civilization.

I know there are men who, in their superciliousness, affect to look down on the labouring man as of a lower order in the scale of being than themselves, and to be treated as inferiors. Though all their supplies of necessary goods as well as their luxuries come to them as the product of labour, they still regard the labourer as occupying a low position. This class do not consider that labour is the lot of mankind, whether in barbarism or civilization, and only under the latter can there be those instrumentalities that make labour efficient—give progress in the affairs of men—dignify industry, and promote the general happiness of men. But that class of capitalists are the exception—the general sentiment in this free country and every country where freedom prevails is, to honor labour. It is only where slavery has debased public sentiment, or when laws or usages have created artificial distinction and privilege, that labour is not respected. In a free country labour will be honored, and no labour that is

performed in a manly and faithful manner, will be dis-
respected by any sensible and honest people.

I have no sympathy with those who seem to take
credit to themselves in complaints of our organization
of labour, and who intimate, if they do not assume,
there is some oppressive wrong on the part of capitalists.   If this idea is traced to its source, it will be
found to be at issue with the right of private property.
And what would there be in this right, if it did not
secure its use to the owner.   If others are to determine it for him, then it must inevitably be wasted ;
the motive for a prudent economy would be lost, and
with it our civilization must be abandoned.   As a
matter of course, the instruments of industry would
pass away, and society would drift into barbarism.   If
the complaint above referred to be sound, then civilization is an evil and our general well-being is not pro-
moted, but injured by its influence, and barbarism is
to be preferred.   That the teaching above referred to
is not more mischievous, arises from the fact that it is
below the plane of our civilization, and is generally regarded as impracticable.   With all the folly that is
manifest, there is still a prevailing number of sensible
people who know that the anticipated possession of a
thing is the stimulus to individual endeavour ; and
endeavour is the prelude to elevation in material and

moral well-being. All efforts that impair such endeavour, take from the working-man the very element
on which his hopes must be founded, and is a demor-
alization, and by no means a process of his elevation.

Let no American working-man, who possesses
health and ordinary powers, feel that his lot is a hard
one. It is in his power to provide for his own well-
being. Put on a manly energy and do not hold yourself indigent, nor consider the capitalist as beyond
your reach. The same power of industrious saving
that made him, will in due time make you a capitalist.
The instruments of your industry, that now belong to
the capitalist, you may make your own. Be careful to
cultivate a love of useful work, whether in regard to
the work itself, or in its results. So far as you succeed
in establishing this doctrine, you will be less tempted
to look after the occupation of your time in frolic
and dissipation, which is a sacrifice of time and means
and also impairs health and character, rendering your
march to future well-being difficult, if it does not destroy your hopes.

Be careful not to be led astray by the popularity
of any proposition from your fellow-workmen. Consider carefully if the thing is wise, and will do you
good. Many men go wrong and have no better excuse
than that others did the same, or that others advised

them. It sometimes requires moral nerve to resist the plausible plea of associates, who, in their ill-directed ardor, are very likely to make a demand on your pride or good feeling in order to enlist you in what may prove their folly, and by no means a measure for your good. The man who carefully studies his own interest, and makes it a rule to weigh well any measure that may be proposed for his action, is not likely to be led astray by ridicule, or false notions of honor. In such matters it is always well to consider the party that offers counsel. If it be one that maintains a sound, discreet character, it is well to listen; but if it be one who loves amusement and idle chat, rather then useful work, it will not profit to accept the advice he may offer. Keep your own counsel.

General Suggestions.

I would like to warn every young man against the error and delusion that may tempt him from the path of honest endeavour in providing for his future well-being. But this is impossible in regard to the numerous details that demand his attention, and will more or less mould his career. Therefore I can only discuss those cardinal principles that may serve as a basis.

With all the preparation he may have, the young man will have much to learn as he moves forward in his personal experience. Many things will occur that he had not thought of, and expose him to errors and disappointments. Professed friends and even real friends, will sometimes advise him unwisely, even when they intend his good. There are many intricacies and troubles in business affairs that can only be well understood from the teachings of personal experience. These admonish caution. The thing may present a plausible aspect, yet the end may not be clear. In any path proposed that you have not fully explored and made satisfactory to your own judgment, proceed with caution and feel your way. In the mean time, " make haste slowly."

There are two things for a young man to keep steadily in view in order to secure success; namely, to fit himself with a thorough knowledge of the art he has chosen for a vocation, and the tact necessary to obtain occupation in the same. In regard to the first, no opportunity should be lost that may improve his skill. This will depend very much upon the thoroughness he has acquired in his apprenticeship. If he has studied well its principles and acquired skilful manipulation in his art, it will not be easy to deceive him by any plausible theory that may be proposed, and he will be able to scan and criticise any proposition and judge if there be anything in it by which he may improve his art or his tools.   He should always be looking and studying for improvement, and to do this wisely or even safely, he must understand well the principles involved in his vocation.   Be cautious of the advice of your fellow-workmen ; not a suspicious caution, but a prudent caution.   Though it may be painful to think so, it is necessary to bear in mind what experience teaches, that some of these will probably go into the dependent class, where I trust it is not your purpose to follow them.   Take no advice that may lead you to waste material, tools or time ; or to impress you with the severity of any irksome feature in the work of your vocation ; but bear in mind there is no vocation that has not something unpleasant in its occupation, and that your decision and energy in overcoming such impediments to your progress is only a necessary discipline to strengthen your energy and purpose and thereby fit you to overcome any obstacle that may oppose your progress. You may also be tempted to seek vain and unprofitable amusements that tend to dissipation and waste—do not heed them, but learn to love the path to the shop, better than the path from it. Be not over-active on the ringing of the bell for vacation.

In regard to the second of the above propositions— " the opportunity for occupation," I remark : As you enter on the field of individual responsibility, it is very possible you may find a scanty opening for employment in your particular vocation. Some peculiarity may restrict the demand, and you do not find ready call for your services. As yet you have had but little opportunity to strengthen your character as a workman. Under such circumstances keep a vigilant eye on all the field in range of your vision. If anywhere an opening appears, though it may be inferior to your expectations, do not fail to embrace it. Once fairly in the harness, you will have opportunity to show what you can do, and now, by your industry and fidelity, so thoroughly perform your work that you will gain character, and though you may receive less wages than your work is worth, you will gain standing in your vocation, and come to be in demand. No one can see far in the future ; but it is obvious a man in work, though it may not be what he is entitled to, stands a far better chance of obtaining the position to which his merits entitle him than one who stands with folded hands outside. A man in the harness is much more likely to attract attention, and gain the employment he seeks and desires, than one who is merely in waiting. On this ground take No. 2 or 3, if you cannot obtain No. 1. In all cases avoid, if possible, an idle waiting, even though some unionist may sneer, call you a black sheep or by other vituperative epithet, with a view to frighten you

13

to decline what it may be your interest to do. In all such attempts on your independence, remember that it usually happens the sneering associate is looking for his own and not your interest. Be your own judge, the law of demand and supply is the only safe standard as established by the market, and it is far better to depend on your own skill and fidelity than on any monopoly that can be formed by Trades Unions.

In the course of invention there is danger that your special vocation may be impaired. This is quite likely to happen in a mill where several classes of mechanics are employed. To fortify yourself against such contingencies, lose no opportunity to notice the manipulation in different departments of work. If you have a good knowledge of mechanical principles, and are well skilled in the use of tools, you will readily appreciate the several kinds of work, and be able with very little practice to do such other work as you may find it your interest to do. It is not necessary for this that you neglect your own work, as there will often be opportunity, especially in the same mill, to notice the operations in other branches than your own. It is very possible this may fit you for continuous work, when your special branch may be superseded by new inventions.

NECESSITY OF EXPERIENCE.

No measure of educational outfit can dispense with personal experience. The latter is a necessary complement of the former. But experience is only obtained by practice and observation in the course of affairs, and this the young working-man has had only limited opportunity to acquire. Practical experience can only be acquired by the personal intercourse of the individual; and much care will be required to so sift out the chaff from the wheat as to make it valuable. If the process be attended with an undue degree of vanity, or high confidence of the young man in his own powers, tending to eschew the experience of others, and hardly profiting by his own, he will probably pass through life in a process of continual blunders, never profiting by even his own experience.

It requires wisdom, and the exercise of a careful, discreet reflection, to profit from even one's own experience. It is far easier to make a mistake than to thoroughly investigate a subject. A man may be largely educated, and this to small purpose, if at the same time he has not had intermingled with his education a sound discipline. I mean by discipline, a habit of carefully scrutinizing any proposition, according to its importance, with the ability to lay aside preconceived views that may have taken possession of the mind, and are very apt to be a barrier to truth. A man should not yield his judgment too readily; he should see there was adequate reason, and after giving a proposition a full hearing, that convinces him of its truth, he will do well to ponder awhile before he makes it the basis of his business action. This is the converse of a careless, easy adoption of a measure, that lacks the moral nerve to make a thorough examination of its merits. No man can expect success in a loose harness; it must be buckled up, so as to take direct hold of the work. This should be carefully considered in all education, as a loose, careless habit, as well as a loose harness, will destroy all hope until it be corrected. It is not all gold that glitters; but it is an established fact, that no work can be well prosecuted, unless the appliances for its manipulation are well appointed and in fitting order.

Elements of Moral Culture.

I do not think I can properly leave this subject without considering the tendency of the human mind to err in regard to moral principle, and improperly yield to the urgency of desire, of passion and appetite. I have endeavoured to set forth the benefits of self-control, and to urge its importance in our civilization—its necessity as an indispensable requisite for the advancement of our well-being, whereby we may obtain the blessings of a sound cultivation. Now I have one more suggestion, in the way of precaution, to fortify the sentiment of a sound morality, which is the basis of all human improvement. It is the question put by the Psalmist, (cxix. 9) " Wherewithal shall a young man cleanse his way?" To this the Psalmist makes answer as follows : " By taking heed thereto according to thy word." It will be understood the word referred to, is the Christian Scriptures. It is not my purpose to make extended remarks on this suggestion ; only to allude to some general principles that bear on the business prosperity and happiness of men.

I think it will not be controverted, these Scriptures are a vast store of searching wisdom, bearing on all the concerns of life. Nowhere can a man find so close and searching a mirror of himself, or of the motives that govern men. In language of unsurpassed terseness and eloquence, in varied and numerous forms, its teaching is unfolded to the understanding so as to show in clear lines, " the light that lighteth every man." They are so plain that no honest man need fail to learn the duty he owes to his Maker, or to his fellow-man. Though they contain things we may not understand, we shall find by careful and honest study that such difficulties will diminish, and there will be found no want of ability for reaching the knowledge above stated.

It is important to keep steadily in view the leading characteristics of these Scriptures, which are to establish and maintain "justice and judgment," righteousness and peace among men. However their meaning may be perverted to give interpretation to favour motives of ambition, it is their great purpose to establish the doctrine of personal responsibility ; and consequently it is the province and the duty of every one to study their teachings for himself. To follow the blind leader is held to be no excuse. It may be replied, these Scriptures relate to a future life, and what has that to do with the question of labour and capital ? No doubt they relate to a future life, but they by no means disregard the life that now is. It is according to Scripture teaching that a wise discharge of the duties of this life is necessary to prepare us for the life to come. But I do not propose to follow this further than to point out the special benefits they afford in establishing a sound social and business character, leaving to every one as they may think proper to consider their influence on a future life.

The Scriptures afford the most varied and explicit rules for defining and enforcing industry, prudence and frugality in affairs—uprightness in all business intercourse; purity and forbearance in manners, and the courtesy, kindness and fellow-feeling that make happiness for the individual and for society, and lay the foundation of civil liberty. They give us such a knowledge of ourselves, and so unfold the springs of human action, that we are able to see more clearly the motives that govern others, and so guard us against deception. By a candid and diligent study of the Scriptures we shall see those tendencies in the human mind that pervert their teaching and lead to errors. They are adapted to all conditions of men, in fact they place all men on the same moral level, and lay the foundation of universal freedom for man, under the safeguards of Institutional law.

I am aware it may be replied,—Some men do not recognize the Divine authority of those Scriptures. I cannot discuss this, but may remark, eminent men, who entertain this doubt, have borne testimony to the high moral excellence of the Scriptures, commending their value in establishing virtue among men. Whatever doubt may be suggested, it cannot be successfully controverted, that the highest rank of civilization, in all historic time, has appeared where the light of the Christian Scriptures has shone most clearly, and where their teaching has been most fully exemplified in the morals

of men. General education, science and the useful
arts—all those charitable institutions that are designed
to ameliorate suffering, and provide for those that are
unable to provide for themselves, are the outgrowth
of the Christian Scriptures, and show in strong light
the superiority of Christian over Pagan civilization.

As to our own country, our Institutional freedom,
our right of conscience, and the unrestricted rights of
labour and protection under law, rest on our training in
principles of civil liberty, as taught in those Scriptures.
They are the foundation of our civilization, and this
will be perfected, as we advance to the more full realiza-
tion and practice of their teachings. They are the
guardian of the rights of the working-man, the only
lever that can raise him to the moral standard
necessary to enable him to make the best improvement
of his faculties, and by these to raise him to the possession of the means of independence and happiness,
giving dignity to his labour, and self-respect in all
his intercourse with his fellow-men.

No young man should fail to study carefully the
Proverbs of Solomon. They show a profound knowl-
edge of business, and wisdom in all the affairs of men.
Taken in connection with the general teaching of
Scripture, they are a rich fund of instruction in all the
affairs that affect the happiness of mankind. The

man who loves civil liberty, and the blessings of Institutional law, will find in the careful study of the Scriptures the firm foundation of whatsoever is just, whatsoever is pure, and of every virtue that can adorn man and give eminent value to the high civilization they inculcate. And these are the fundamental principles that secure to all men the blessings of freedom. In all the affairs of life, in individual, social and political duties, he will realize the value of the advice quoted from the Psalmist—" taking heed thereto according to thy word."

Some men claim that they are the only authorized interpreters of Scripture, and that it is dangerous for common men to undertake the reading, except under their guidance. The great apostle expressed approval of men who searched the Scriptures to ascertain whether he gave the correct interpretation. No doubt various interpretations are made by different men, and these men of high attainments and ability, who may be regarded as having equal authority. But if the apostle was right, then the layman should examine for himself, and be able to judge which interpretation was the most faithful representation of Scripture truth. There doubtless is some Scripture it may be difficult or even impossible to understand. This may be inferred from the varied conclusions of

learned Doctors in theology, who may be equally entitled to respect.   But the precept, "Thou shalt not
steal," and numerous others of equal simplicity and
importance, will be readily understood by all honest
minds.

In the above remarks, I by no means intend any
disrespect towards the teachers of religion ; would
rather listen with respectful attention to their interpretations and teaching.   I regard them as of eminent
value in inculcating the great moral truths of Scripture.
But I regard it as of equal importance, that those who
listen be so well instructed in the knowledge of
Scripture truth, as to be able to distinguish, whether
the teacher is labouring for the shell or the kernel.

The Scripture does not say *ye* shall not steal, but
thou shalt not steal.   After having read the Scriptures
with considerable attention for more than half a century, I have reached the conclusion, that they address
us as individuals, demanding personal attention and
obedience to their commands ; and on this basis they
devolve the personal obligation on each one, to study
their teachings, and be guided as under a call for
individual duty !   Indeed this idea is amply inculcated
in the Scriptures, as devolving on each one the duty
of studying for one's self, and declaring that they are
so plain, " the wayfaring man " may understand all

that is necessary for the discharge of his religious duties. I do not mean by this, that there are no social duties, for it will be found these are all embraced in individual duty, as the same are beautifully unfolded in this great system of moral government.

I have not introduced this subject as a theologian, but as a layman, after having reached the conclusion that the Christian Scriptures are eminently beneficent in their influence on the business affairs of men. They include the stern justice that protects the weak, and maintains to all equal rights of labour, of conscience and political freedom, " To keep the way of the Lord, to do justice and judgment." They have produced the highest civilization the world has known, and especially in establishing Institutional law, for the maintenance of freedom and the just rights of men. Every working-man (and we are mostly of this class) should regard them as the constitution of his rights in all the affairs of business, of society and of civil liberty.

All the scientific writers on industrial economy that I have seen, agree in the opinion, it is the cultivation of the moral in men that must be relied on to raise them to the best use of their powers. I think this sentiment cannot be successfully controverted. If, then, it be conceded that our progress in civilization, or the general elevation of society, depends on our growth in moral character, the teaching of the Scriptures must be regarded as highly valuable, if not indispensable to that progress. In one respect it must be held the Scripture is peculiarly influential on the masses of men—namely, that it adds to the wisdom of its precepts the force of a Divine sanction. To its precepts it adds, " do this and live."

Whatever may be claimed for any systems of morals that have been wrought out and presented to the world by human wisdom, they have produced comparatively very small influence on the order, justice, purity and general happiness of mankind, as compared to what has been accomplished by Scripture culture. In connection with education, the Scriptures are our reliance for enlarging and beautifying our civilization in all that can elevate and adorn our manhood, and so reducing the ratio of the dependent to the independent class of men. This is not all: as we improve the material and moral well-being of society, we shall diminish the criminal class, and with it the large expenses involved in protecting society from their depredations. As we advance in moral culture, men will " cease to do evil and learn to do well."

I believe in the doctrine of the providence of God ruling over all the affairs of men in righteousness and truth. At the same time I hold, that according to Scripture teaching, the Divine rule is so ordered and administered, as in a proper sense to leave men in the control of their own destiny. This is manifest in the experience of men. Those who, in an abiding faith in the authority of the Scriptures, and in obedience to their teaching, practice diligent industry, prudence, uprightness and purity of life, are found to constitute the great bulk of the independent class. On the other hand, the dependent class are mostly made up of men who are wanting in some, if not all those virtues.

I therefore say to the young working-man, your destiny is not a matter of chance, it is a matter of purpose, left in your own hands to decide which class you will fall into. God will aid you, when you put your shoulder to the wheel, and with manly effort overcome the impediments that may appear in your path. This is the main question, and it can only be decided by yourself. The benefit, no less than the responsibility, rest with you. If you have not the moral nerve to meet it affirmatively—and prefer a loose, indolent waste of your powers, you must eventually take your place in the ranks of dependent men. There is no escape from this.

However men may be degraded to a love of low

pleasures, and come to disrespect all else, there can be no doubt the moral is what gives the noble characteristics of our being ; and surely we shall be elevated, as we progress in the formation of the cardinal virtues, that give eminence, and adorn our civilization.

It should be our hope and joy that we live under the reign of Institutional law, founded on the basis of Scripture morality, whereby every man is free in the exercise of all his powers of industry and virtue, and at the same time protected against any that would assail his right, or impair his success. The power of every man is his own property, and when exercised with discretion and energy, it will redound to his benefit and honour. The true and legitimate advance of moral culture, will work an amelioration that can be found in no other way. It will tend to modify, if it does not remove, all ground for contest in this question of labour and capital.

Instruments and Labour.

I cannot dismiss this subject without calling the attention of working-men to the benign agency that has put in their hands the instruments that have vastly increased their power. This has been referred to incidentally in the preceding pages ; but I desire to be somewhat more explicit. It is proper to consider, these instruments have not resulted from accident, nor from any arbitrary action of men. They have been sought for the purpose of alleviating the severity and increasing the effectiveness of labour. They have been the product of many intelligent men, who by slow degrees, in the application of their minds to invent, and by persistent perseverance in manipulation of the varied parts—patiently varying their operations as indicated by experiment, until a form had been reached and so combined as to meet the object they desired. Now, it is important to consider the object they had in view. What was it? It was to mitigate the more severe toil and increase the facility of manipulation in fabricating the goods that are called for by the wants of men ; to reduce manual labour by substituting mechanical agents and brute force to perform the work that had been done by men ; and so provide a more easy production of articles needed ; and also to do works that manual power had not been able to accomplish.

The result of these instruments has greatly changed the characteristics of labour. What before was either not produced at all, or was produced by manual labour, is now in great measure the labour of mechanical agents or brute force. They have not removed the necessity of manual labour, but have taken away in large measure the more painful toil, and given it a more watchful and skilled character, whereby a man exercises his body more lightly, and finds employment for his mind.   This latter is very important as giving a man an interest in thought, that greatly alleviates the toil of manipulation ; giving the pleasure of mind, as co-operating in production, mitigating the severity of continued manual effort, and so giving pleasurable occupation, by uniting the action of the body and mind in a manner that relieves the severity of toil, and so escaping much of the drudgery of the old process.

As suggested, it does not render labour unnecessary, but provides a cheaper and easier process of fabrication ; that is, to make goods more plenty, and thereby bring the cost within the means of a larger number of men. In the changes that have been made by improved methods of industry, there has no doubt resulted more or less of inconvenience to the labourer, who has found his old trade superseded, and he compelled to resort to some other occupation, or adapt himself to the new method of work.   This must be admitted as an evil ; but I see no remedy, as mankind will seize every improved method that cheapens commodities, and the labourer must be exposed to the risk of such improvements as may interfere with any special occupation.   This view is in many cases relieved by the facility which the new method affords of employment by the same workmen that were occupied in the old method; the change not being such that the former workmen may not adapt themselves to the new requirements.

While it must be admitted the changes above referred to have some deranging influence on labour, there can be no doubt the volume of labour has been greatly increased by the improved instruments that have been provided. The reason for this is found in the fact that by cheapening commodities, consumption is increased. This is what gives the public favour to all improved methods of production. The inventor may, or may not, regard the public good; but that is not material to the question, as the main thing here considered is the effect of improved methods of labour on the interests of society. In this view they are the legitimate production of civilization—a continual striving to effect the most economical production. However the man that sees his occupation disturbed, may relish the innovation, or have a claim for sympathy, the public will always hail with satisfaction any new method by which supplies may be cheapened.

That the above view is a correct interpretation of public sentiment, is manifest from the action of governments in granting letters patent to inventors for a term of years, during which they are secured in the exclusive right of their invention. Until the term has expired, the public has no right to the use of the invention. That this action of governments is founded on the idea that improved methods of production are a public benefit, there can be no doubt. Every nation strives to perfect its own facilities, in order to enter in the most favourable way into the competitions of other nations, in all the industries it is adapted to prosecute. It is obvious, other things being equal, the nation that has the most intelligent and ingenious people, will control the largest amount of productive industry. Consequently they will be able to maintain the largest commerce, and support the most dense population.

The progress of ingenuity within the last century has introduced and brought into successful operation an amount of improved methods, that have revolutionized productive industry. No intelligent man would thing of going back to former methods. As a people we have gradually accommodated ourselves to this new and improved order of industry. In cheapening the cost of commodities, it has given enlarged consumption—extending to numerous members of society, articles of living they had not previously enjoyed, besides furnishing necessary articles for men at a reduced cost.

This is the condition of industry that makes large demands for the instruments of labour. It is a condition in which the labourer cannot do without the instruments, and the instruments can only be had by the saving that results from abstinence. This abstinence is the frugal husbanding of the proceeds of labour, and is stimulated by an appreciation of its value in the future. The instrument so secured by the prudent abstinent, is simply another term for capital. It was obtained by persistent saving in order to secure the benefit of its use in the hands of the abstinent, or with a view to loan it for a consideration to those who had not saved it. After invention, the instrument is merely the result of prudent labour, and is entitled to its pay, on precisely the same basis, that a man is entitled to pay for his work. They are alike work, and stand on equal terms as to right of remuneration. There is no possible difference in the rights of these parties. The compensation is in both cases for labour—though one be preferred for a present object, and the other through abstinence for the present to secure a future object; they are equally the product of labour, and enter on the list of free trade between the parties, the same as any commodities should do.

The labourer needs the instruments, for their necessity has become incorporated in the existing civilization, and it would be in vain that he look for sources of industry that did not require them. In any effort that should dispense with the instruments, the labourer would be impotent; while with their use, labour would be more productive to the labourer as well as to the public. No man can have the instruments unless he is willing to provide them, or if he has not provided them, he should pay the man who has saved them, a proper interest or benefit for their use. On this principle the whole order of our business civilization rests, and it cannot be disturbed by any process that does not lead to barbarism. Some regard this view as a hardship to labour, which is simply a plea that the prudent abstinent shall divide his earnings with the improvident, who chose to consume their earnings, and have left nothing for saving.

The fact of the existence of the instruments, that are in readiness for the labourer, is a vast benefit to him; greatly enlarging the field of his labour, and giving him the power, if he has the requisite abstinence, to provide them for himself. He has the experience before him of the practicability of doing this, from the large numbers who have by a course of prudent industry accumulated their own instruments. These instruments which I have described, are only another name for capital. The question, therefore, if

there be any contest, is between the instruments and
the labour, that is performed by their means, and
which could not be performed without them.

It is obvious the preceding remarks are not necessary to convince intelligent men; but I am writing
with a view of benefiting young working-men; a very
large class, to which our young men mostly belong.
In their inexperience they are liable to be misled on
a question in which they are deeply interested. It is
sought in various ways to impress on their minds
several erroneous notions; as that labour is oppressed—
that it is weak—that in its impotence it is unable to
provide for itself, and should in some way have aid to
relieve its burdens. In regard to all this, if we did
not enjoy civil liberty, and our society was divided
into classes, in which the mass of men were made to
contribute a large share of their earnings to the
support of a privileged class, there would be some
ground for those claims, which are held to be philanthropic. But this is by no means our situation. We
are a free people, and such classes as we have are
what they have made themselves by the legitimate
exercise of their own personality, in the same field
that was alike open to all men. We know no law of
entail or privilege; every man is free to use his powers
as he thinks will best promote his own interest. All

labourers have the dignity of unrestricted manhood, with full and free scope for their endeavours. They stand on an independent basis, the basis of freedom, with the right and the power to exercise themselves for their own benefit, and every one can take such course of industry as he regards most likely to promote his own welfare, with a reasonable certainty of finding a market for his skill and labour. The instruments civilized liberty has put into his hands are eminently superior to those of any previous age—are a great boon to the labourers of the present day, and only demand a manly energy to make them successful in providing a competent independence.

It must not be forgotten that every able-bodied young man is in duty bound to provide for his own well-being. He has no right to expect another will work for him gratuitously, any more than he will expect to give his own services without compensation. If his neighbour has provided the instruments he needs, he should expect to pay for their use according to their market value. They increase his power of production, and open up a larger field for his labour than could otherwise exist. As surely as he makes the instruments a means of abstinence, and so gathers them for himself, he will expect most rightfully a profit for their use. The latter is the motive for saving; and it is one that has been and will continue to be efficient to every man who has the moral nerve to be a man. The man who lacks such motive is certainly to be pitied for his imbecility, but has no other claim to sympathy.

This whole subject resolves itself into a question of manliness. If this is sufficient to overcome the imbecility that weak minds are prone to indulge, in raising impediments and forming excuses, the young man will steadily rise in his condition, and will soon learn that capital and labour have no contest that is not common in all exchanges for services or goods.

Everything a man works for has a value that arises from desire, and whether this be for present or future use, is immaterial—it may be for bread, or it may be for instruments to improve his production; in either case he labours for the article, and is entitled to the product, and to such appropriation of the proceeds as he judges best for his interest. In the case of the instruments he has begun to be a capitalist in precisely the same way that most capitalists have been made, whether they have been employed in mental or manual labour, or in both combined.

I am well aware the preceding remarks are hardly less or more than truisms, and am far from claiming originality; and have only designed to put them in

216 THE QUESTION OF LABOUR AND CAPITAL.

order as best I could, for the purpose of leading to
reflection on matters that young men are very liable
to regard in a light way, if they do not entirely over-
look. I am very sure they often neglect them, notwithstanding they are matters that deeply concern
their welfare. If our civilization makes useful progress, it must certainly be developed in reducing the
ratio of the dependent class, and also that of the
criminal class. We shall not progress by declaiming
against our civilization, as organized for carrying forward our productive industry; but by elevating the
moral and mental standard and thereby bringing the
animal proclivities of our natures into subordination
to reason and right, and so direct them to the legitimate purposes for which they were ordained.